A Call to Courage

Defeating the Dysfunction
That Holds Your Princess Captive

A Call to Courage

Defeating the Dysfunction That Holds Your Princess Captive

by
Roger Petersohn

Published by
LULU

ISBN: 978-0-557-46879-9

Dedicated to

Sue
*Thank you for your love and patience
as I discover and fight my dragons.*

Appreciation Note

My deep gratitude goes to Dr. Rick Walston, president of Columbia Evangelical Seminary, for his encouragement, proofreading, and editing. (However, any and all errors that you might find in this book are my sole responsibility.)

Table of Contents

Introduction

What you need to know about me and my perspective in order to get the most out of this book.

In the 1990s we saw a fad develop and fade through our TV sets. It was the marriage-improvement infomercial. They had the right idea: offer a quick solution to a big problem, sell a DVD series and a book, and everyone is happy!

From the perspective of turning fifty several months ago, I can see now that the programs were, for the most part, sound, but they didn't deal with the motivation needed to *do* the improved behavior. The concept of the *behavior* being the problem is wrong. Think of it this way, if a woman loves flowers, then all a man has to do is to bring flowers home every day, or every week, correct? Every woman would say "no." A popular movie that came out a few years ago put it this way, the woman speaking to the man: "I want you to *want* to do the dishes!" And there is the key.

A woman can tell if a man is doing the dishes because he has to or because he wants to. And that is the problem. The man doesn't instinctively want to do the dishes because at his core he instinctively wants what *he* wants. The man simply cares about himself more than he cares about the woman. The motivation to do something purely for our wives' pleasure or enjoyment is simply not there. So the flowers show up each day, and they mean nothing.

This book is about finding the ability and courage to care more about your wife than you care about yourself. This book is about finding the strength and courage to care more about communication than you care about sex. This book is about helping you find your wife's laughter again, and, with it, finding the reason why you married her, and with that, finding the heartbeat of your marriage again.

Most men automatically fall into a rut of thinking they simply need to find that right thing to do, to say, to learn, or to change, in order to fix the problem. It is not a matter of a single thing to change. It is a matter of healing the source of all of those things. The heart is the wellspring of life. Everything you say and the tone in which you say it comes from the heart. If the heart is unhealthy, most things coming out of it will be unhealthy. If the heart is healthy, the opposite will be true.

Again, there is not just one thing that needs to be fixed or learned or changed. But there is one central core thing that needs to be healed. And then everything that flows out of it will be better.

This book is about my journey of injury, discovery, and healing. It's about how I had decided not to feel the lows of life as a kid and in the process shut down my ability to feel much at all.

This book is about having the courage to look back into your past and to tear down the wall that you built around your heart, allowing you to feel, love, and live again.

This book is about developing a healthy heart and, with it, the courage to look forward and to start doing those scary things that life and love demand.

Let's get started by making sure that we are on the same page with a few things.

Defining the Heart

What the Bible exactly means when it uses the word "heart" is a somewhat debatable issue. In this book, when I use the word "heart," I am referring to that part of your psyche that includes your mind, your will, and your emotions. As you will clearly see in chapter 2, it *includes* the brain and the emotions, but it goes way beyond them.

Defining Dysfunction

In this book, the word "dysfunction" is used to describe a person's inability to function normally in a relationship situation. These unhealthy behaviors are usually caused by difficult experiences that the person adapts to, usually by withdrawing from relationships, or by responding defensively or harshly.

For clarity, I believe that every person on this planet has dysfunctional behavior. The question is how many dysfunctions do we have and how intense are they? No one was raised by perfect parents or in a perfect environment.

In the 1970s it was a huge social stigma to be labeled dysfunctional, and the counseling that was usually prescribed labeled you as a freak. Today, being dysfunctional is understood to be common (perhaps, ironically, even normal). Furthermore, counseling is now seen as something that a wise and strong person would take advantage of. Thank God!

Self Analysis

This book demands that you have an ability to think through your behavior from a standpoint that considers the possibility of wrongdoing on your part. This process of self-awareness, or self-evaluation, goes back to Socrates who said, "the unexamined life is not worth living."

I wholeheartedly agree. But I find that most people seek to understand their behavior and thought processes from an "explaining" angle, not an "understanding" angle. The *explaining* angle starts with a "yeah, but…" sentence. They seek to explain why their behavior was correct or not as bad as it appears. The *understanding* angle begins with the assumption that they could have done something better. This is precisely what we are looking for. In the physical world, healing normally begins only after an accurate diagnosis, not before. The same is true here.

This has nothing to do with beating yourself up for wrong behavior. I am talking about an honest inward look to improve one's self. This is a powerful tool for change, and essential for healing dysfunction and building a great marriage.

Was That You God?

In this book I will refer to hearing God's voice or His prompting. My experience and study have led me to these conclusions about hearing God's voice:

- God's voice will not come from the clouds but from the Holy Spirit who lives in our hearts. This means that hearing God's voice will sound like a thought that comes to you from within.

- Since our flesh is constantly warring against the Holy Spirit inside of us (Galatians 5:17-23), we can assume that any thought that is *not* evil could be the Holy Spirit. If it is not evil, and it is not God, but rather from last night's pepperoni pizza, we haven't lost anything.

- The follow-thru is crucial. Hearing God's voice is of no value if you disregard His instruction. True, He may just tell you that He loves you and no response beyond gratitude is needed. But when you feel His nudge to go a certain direction, going is a must or it shuts the whole process down.

- God will reward your *attempts* to hear His voice not just your successes. Hebrews 11:6 tells us that he rewards those who seek Him, not just find Him. I have found this process to be like learning another language. It feels very awkward at first but becomes easier and more successful with time.

You will need the assurance of God's presence with you in order to persevere through this journey. Hearing His voice will give you the assurance of His presence and will bring with it His strength. So listen for His voice. Begin to expect His involvement and His thoughts because He loves the fact that you are considering this endeavor.

A Valid Study

There are hundreds of verses in the Bible that tell of the heart's value and involvement in our lives. But it doesn't seem to tell us much about healing or guarding our heart, at least not directly. The temptation, therefore, might be to discount this concept. I encourage you to consider the example of the Great Commission found in Matthew 28:18-20. Jesus tells us to go into all the world and to make disciples. But He does not tell us how, specifically. He doesn't tell us the order of the countries to go into, nor the organizational structure to develop it under, nor a million other details that would help us in the process of carrying out the Great Commission. I guess God, in all His wisdom, decided that we needed to figure some things out for ourselves. Perhaps the answer would be different for each generation. Perhaps the exercise of figuring it out would be good for us. Who knows? All we know is that we are told to do it, so we have to figure it out.

Perhaps the same is true here. We can stand on the truth that the heart is central to life. In this we do have clear scriptural instruction (see next chapter). From there we seek to understand its role, to guard it, or to begin to heal it if it is broken.

Your Issues Versus My Issues

Since this book comes primarily from my experience with God and His word, it may come across fairly harsh. But, please understand that I do not mean for it to be harsh toward you. In dealing with myself, I find straightforwardness to be essential. If I start fuzzing up the edges of an issue, I'll end up blaming someone else, or letting the urgency slip away, and with it the focus needed to deal with it. My goal in being straightforward is not to be harsh. I am simply trying to convey clearly the messages flying through my heart and head. My issues are not necessarily your issues, and the severity of my issues may not be the severity of your issues. Please see my aggressive writing style as a desire to be clear and uncluttered.

Grace is Our Anchor

I spent most of my adult life beating myself up for not being consistent enough in Bible study and prayer. I figured that if I wasn't consistent enough then I didn't truly love God. And that led me to conclude that He was probably frustrated with me, and perhaps even angry.

We all know that is horrible theology and that the truth is the opposite, but does your heart know it for sure? Does your heart understand that you are loved and accepted as God's child regardless of your behavior? As we talk about battles and being strong and finding victory, please understand that we are working on these things in order to improve the way we think and behave. We are *not* working on these things to get Him on our side and somehow get onto His good list. If your biggest struggle is accepting and enjoying God's love and forgiveness I suggest you read a different book on grace and get that straightened out first.

What Courage Can't Guarantee

This is a book about finding courage and growing a great marriage, but there are no promises for the second part of that sentence. I can promise you that courage is available to you because that depends only on you and God. The great marriage part also depends on your wife, and that is beyond your control. But I do believe this with all my heart; the vast majority of women want to fully love their husbands and to have a truly great marriage.

The temptation here is to figure out how to fix her. Ephesians 5:25-27 clearly tells us that our job, as seen in the role of Christ, is to die to ourselves and to meet our wife's needs, not fix her flaws. With 100% of our effort we are to work on being the best husband possible. This leaves no percentage of our time to focus on what our wives need to change. None, zero, nada!

But here is the beautiful part. Seeing us focus on ourselves and working solely on our issues is the fuel they need to begin wrestling with their issues. We fuel up our wives to grow by focusing completely on our growth! We only completely die to ourselves when we make it our goal to fix 100% of our issues. That's when we look most like Christ. And that's when we begin to inspire our wives in God's direction.

This move toward courage has to be about changing you. Not about fixing your wife. She will sniff that out and it will all be over. But if she is convinced that it is your primary goal to fix *your* issues, I believe you will begin to see miracles.

Accountability Partners

This is not a book about accountability. This is not a book about finding someone to call every time you slip into sin, or are about to. That is a very valid topic and practice, but that's not what this book is about.

This book is about finding the courage to wrestle with the underlying sources of sin hidden deep within us, not simply the struggle with individual sins. This book wrestles with the disease inside our hearts and not the symptoms we see on the surface.

What Dad Didn't Say

My memories of my dad are split, some good and some bad. It seems like he was either laughing or angry. He taught me to play sports and to swing a hammer. He also taught me how to respond to difficulty by getting angry and going on the offensive. He didn't mean to, but he did. And, odds are, he learned that very same thing from his dad.

Dad is 82 now, and my respect for him is greater than it's ever been. He has had some difficult situations come up this past year and has shown a tenderness and courage I never thought I'd see. True, courage at 82 looks different than courage at 52, but courage is courage. I am proud of you dad, and I love you.

Many young men didn't have dads there to tell them that they had the stuff to be strong and capable men. Many of those young men turned to women to find answers and to fill those gaps. But a woman was never meant to answer those questions. A square peg will never fit into a round hole. If our fathers missed the mark, it then becomes

God's job to fill that gap. I believe this process of healing our heart and developing courage is God's way of helping us see our strength to love, to protect, to build up, and to lead. During this process God wants to looks us square in the eye and assure us that we have the stuff it takes to be great men.

May God bless you in this journey! And may you hear Him say, even *before* you get to heaven, "well done, my good and faithful and courageous son!"

Let's get started!

PART ONE: THE PROBLEM

Chapter 1

The Prince Has Lost His Courage

The princess loves the prince because he is brave,
not because he is handsome.
The key ingredient is courage.

I like to think of myself as a man's man. I loved math in school. I lettered three years in golf and took 2nd in state in wrestling my senior year. I have been married for almost 20 years, and Sue and I have 3 kids. I completely remodeled our house, myself, from top to bottom. I tore out walls, I rebuilt new walls, I wired them and hung the sheetrock. I love to fix things and my two greatest accomplishments are a clothes washer and a hot tub.

I am a pastor in a medium size church and am in charge of the music. When it's my turn to lead, I do it in a manly way. I don't like shopping and I struggle in long conversations with my wife about small details.

I am shoring up your mental picture of me because I am going to take a small risk and tell you that I enjoyed fairy tales when I was a kid. There, I said it. Confession is absolutely good for the soul.

Seriously, almost all children are drawn to those fairy tales and the reason for their popularity and longevity is clear. They are written with the deeper things of life and human experience in mind. Especially through those two main characters that we find over and over, in one form or another, the prince and the princess.

In my childhood, those fairy tales initially played the role of entertainment. I now see that they played a much bigger role, that of my first heroes. They were truly written with a deep understanding of what men and women desire to be and to do.

Today's TV shows would have you believe that the deepest thing that a man looks for in a woman is her looks and attitude toward sex. TV would have you believe that the deepest thing a woman looks for in a man is a party attitude and a cute smile. It doesn't take much of a brain to see that the fairy tales were closer to reality than today's average sitcom.

The fairy tales have a theme that you will find in nearly every piece of dramatic writing, that of overcoming adversity. In nearly every serious movie, book, or play, the "hero" must overcome a difficult situation. When the hero rises to the occasion and courageously overcomes the challenge, we are drawn toward that person. We applaud, we tear up, we smile, we are entertained, and we identify (or at least we want to).

We've all watched sporting events where the better team kills the lesser team from beginning to end. How entertaining was that? You may have enjoyed it if your favorite team was the winning team, but honestly, did it entertain you? Did it keep you on the edge of your seat? Did you jump up and celebrate wildly at any point? You probably didn't. In fact, rather than watching the game with any kind of intensity, you probably ended up having light-hearted conversations with others around you.

But think back to the New England Patriots/New York Giants Super Bowl game back in January, 2007. Will you ever forget that catch that David Tyree made on that final scoring drive, clutching the ball to his helmet? Do you remember your reaction when he made the catch? Odds are you were on your feet yelling or cheering wildly for or against him. He came through adversity, and whether you loved the Patriots or the Giants, you were glued to your TV sets.

In your brain, right now, try to come up with a movie or book that doesn't have that concept at its core. The hero overcomes his fear or his adversity and defeats the villain. The underdog trains hard and defeats the pro. The bumbling idiots get it together and become a team. The less-than-handsome boy wins the heart of the beauty. The average person has an opportunity to be the hero and does what needs to be done. Maybe I need to broaden my entertainment vault a bit but that single theme of overcoming adversity seems to permeate nearly every area of entertainment that I enjoy.

In the process of the hero overcoming adversity, we weren't simply entertained, we were drawn toward the hero. We were drawn to respect him, to appreciate him, or to care about him. We didn't just want to clap but we wanted him to *hear* us clap. We wanted him to know we appreciated what he did, what he accomplished. And that is why the princess loves the prince.

Get this picture in your mind. A beautiful princess is being held captive by her enemy in an evil tower. The tower is being guarded by a dragon. The hero is poised to rescue the princess but has to defeat the dragon first. The princess is in the tower window calling to the prince and watching his every move. The question is, "What will the prince choose to do?"

What are his options? Well, he can risk his life and fight for this particular princess or go find one that doesn't have a dragon standing in the way. What does the prince do? He chooses to fight for *this* princess. And that is what wins the heart of the princess. She falls in love with the prince because he chooses to fight for *her*. He is not forced to, but he chooses to. Granted, he has seen the beauty of the princess but he still has to decide if he will risk his life for her.

We are not just talking about the basic elements of entertainment, but the basic elements of love and relationship. Think back to what Christ did for us. He came for us, and died for us, by choice. He loved us, by choice. He obeyed the Father, and gave His life on a cross, for us, by choice. And if we allow them to, those truths will draw us back to His heart every day.

There is a key ingredient present in Christ, in the prince, and in our entertainment heroes, but perhaps missing in us. That ingredient is courage. Our entertainment heroes have the courage to...

- Get up before dawn, daily, and train for the big fight.
- Stand up for what is right and face embarrassment.
- Stand between the bully and the small kid and perhaps take a beating.
- Look deep into themselves and make some major changes.
- Risk losing everything they have for a cause more valuable.
- Work and think hard enough to find the non-obvious answer.

Let's Begin With Some Self Analysis

Courage is necessary to fight the dragon. Courage is necessary to rescue the princess. Courage is necessary to give the princess her smile back. How are you doing in this area of courage? Imagine a line drawn from left to right across this page. The word, "comfortable" is written on the left edge of the page and the word "courageous" is written on the right side. Where on that line would you put yourself on a normal day when it comes to your relationship with your wife?

If you put yourself in the middle somewhere, list some of the things that you do to intentionally show courage each day. List the things that scare you, but you intentionally do them anyway. Would it be easier to list the things you do that are comfortable? Do you want to adjust your place on the line?

In his book, *Marriage Builder*, Larry Crabb says that at any given time we are either manipulating our wives or ministering to them. Imagine a second line across our page with "manipulating" on the left side and "ministering to" on the right. Again, where on that line would you put yourself on a normal day? List the things that you do to intentionally minister to her needs. Would it be easier to list the things that you do that are manipulative at any level? Does your placement need adjusting?

Is it any wonder that our wives aren't smiling like they used to? Is it any wonder they don't seem to instantly love and respect us like they used to? Is it any wonder we aren't as thrilled with the relationship as we once were?

I am afraid that most men, including myself, are on the "comfortable" end of the spectrum. Everything about "comfortable" and "manipulate" come natural for me. The other two, well . . . you get my point. I want to be courageous but it feels like trying to talk in a foreign language. Paul's words in Romans 7 ring especially true when I line them up next to my courage scale. "I know the good things I ought to do, but I don't do them. I know the bad things I shouldn't do, but those are the things I do."

But, now here's the clincher guys . . . are you ready for this? You are your wife's potential prince. You are the man God put in her life to fulfill that role. If you want to find the courage to defeat the dragon and win your princess' smile back, I have some great news for you. And it doesn't come in the form of some lofty spiritual mindset. It takes place right here on the ground where our hands can touch it, and our feet can step on it.

But before we go down that road, let's take a look at the "home of courage," that place where courage resides, your heart.

Discussion Questions for Chapter 1

Who were some of your childhood heroes? What strength or quality did they display that inspired you?

What are a few of your favorite movies? Is "overcoming adversity" a theme anywhere in them? How do those parts of the movie impact you or make you feel?

Where did you place yourself on the two lines? Do you agree with the statement that the lines are related to each other? Did you find yourself wanting to fudge the truth a bit?

What is your goal in reading this book?

Chapter 2

The Heart of the Problem

Healthy heart, healthy relationships.
Injured heart, injured relationships.

Above all else, guard the heart,
For it affects everything you do.
Proverbs 4:23

Most men hear the word "heart" and instantly think of emotional stuff and see it primarily as a female quality or issue. We couldn't be more wrong. The Bible would call the heart the deepest part of a man *or* a woman, the most vital part.

Listen to the centrality of the heart according to the Bible and notice how it pertains to both men and women. Take careful note of the fact that being a "man's man" demands having those things that a healthy man's heart is supposed to have and do and give.

- Leviticus 19:17 shows us that the <u>heart</u> is the home of hatred.
- Leviticus 26:41 tells us that the <u>heart</u> is the part of us that is either stubborn or humble.
- In Deuteronomy 5:29 God says that the <u>heart</u> is where He wants to do the bulk of His work.
- In Deuteronomy 6:5 we are instructed to love the Lord our God with all our <u>heart</u>, soul and strength.
- Deuteronomy 7:7 points to God's <u>heart</u> as the place where He decides and determine things.
- Deuteronomy 9:4 says that the <u>heart</u> is the place where we deceive ourselves.
- Deuteronomy 10:16 shows us that stubbornness lives in the <u>heart.</u>
- Deuteronomy 11:16 says that turning away from God begins with a deception in the <u>heart.</u>

- Deuteronomy 20:3 tells us that our <u>heart</u> is the home of our courage.

- Deuteronomy 30:1 tells us that the <u>heart</u> is where we do our deepest thinking.

- In Deuteronomy 30:14, the <u>heart</u> is the key to obedience.

- Joshua 23:14 says that deep in your <u>heart</u> is where you know something is true.

- In 1 Samuel 4:13 we see that the <u>heart</u> is the home of fear.

- 2 Samuel 3:21 says that the <u>heart</u> is the home of our desires.

- In 2 Samuel 15:6 Absalom stole the <u>hearts</u> of all the people (their devotion).

- In 1 Kings 3:9 Solomon asks for an understanding <u>heart</u> so that he may be wise.

- 1 Kings 11:4 tells us that the <u>heart</u> is the home of worship.

- 2 Chronicles 16:9 tells us that the Lord loves to strengthen those whose <u>hearts</u> are fully committed to him.

- Nehemiah 2:12 shows us that when God speaks to a man it is to his <u>heart.</u>

- In Job 22:22, the <u>heart</u> is the home of a person's memory.

- In Job 29:13, the <u>heart</u> is the home of joy.

- In Job 31:9, the <u>heart</u> is the home of lust.

- In Psalm 16:7 we find that even at night, David's <u>heart</u> instructs him.

- Psalm 26:2 tells us that our motives are found in our <u>heart.</u>

- We see in Psalm 73:21 that the <u>heart</u> can become bitter.

- In Psalm 102:3 David's distress is described as a sick <u>heart</u>, withered like grass.

- Psalm 109:22 says the <u>heart</u> can be full of pain.

- Psalm 119:11 says we find strength to not sin by hiding God's Word in our <u>heart.</u>

- In Psalm 131:1 the <u>heart</u> is the home of pride.

- In Proverbs 3:5 the <u>heart</u> is the home of our ability to trust.

- Proverbs 11:20 says the <u>heart</u> is the home of integrity.

- In Proverbs 14:13 we find that the <u>heart</u> is the home of grief.
- In Proverbs 14:30 a peaceful <u>heart</u> leads to a healthy body.
- Proverbs 27:19 says that the <u>heart</u> reflects the real person.
- In Ecclesiastes 3:11 Solomon tells us that our desire for eternal things is planted in our <u>heart.</u>
- In Song of Solomon 4:9 the man's <u>heart</u> is ravished by the beauty of his lover.
- Isaiah 57:15, we repent in our <u>heart.</u>
- Isaiah 62:1, we yearn in our <u>heart.</u>
- Isaiah 66:2, humility lives in the <u>heart.</u>
- Isaiah 66:14, rejoicing begins in the <u>heart.</u>
- In Jeremiah 17:10 the <u>heart</u> is labeled as the home of our secret motives.
- Malachi 2;15-16, guarding your <u>heart</u> is linked to being faithful to your wife.
- In Matthew 5:8 Jesus tells us that those whose <u>hearts</u> are pure will see God.
- Matthew 9:4, the <u>heart</u> is the home of evil thoughts.
- Matthew 12:34, whatever is in your <u>heart </u>determines what you will say.
- In Matthew 15:19 we are told that evil thoughts, murder, adultery, all sexual immorality, theft, lying, and slander come out of the <u>heart.</u>
- Mark 7:15, we are defiled by what comes out of the <u>heart.</u>
- Mark 11:23, the <u>heart</u> is where we doubt.
- In Luke 2:19 Mary pondered the angel's message in her <u>heart.</u>
- Luke 12:34 tells us that our treasures will always show us where our <u>heart </u>is.
- John 14:27, the <u>heart</u> is the home of peace.
- In Acts 5:3 Ananias and Sapphira sin and are killed after Satan filled their <u>heart.</u>
- In Romans 10:9,10 we are clearly told that the <u>heart</u> is where we believe and are saved.

- 2 Corinthians 1:22, the Holy Spirit lives in our <u>hearts</u> when we become a Christian.

- 2 Corinthians 5:12, the <u>heart</u> is the home of our sincerity.

- In Colossians 3:15 we are instructed to let Christ's peace rule in our <u>hearts.</u>

- James 3:14, selfishness lives in the <u>heart.</u>

Pretty overwhelming list, huh? Proverbs 4:23 tells us that the heart is the wellspring of life, the core of what makes us alive, productive, and satisfied. After reading through that list we can clearly see that it is true. It's no wonder that Solomon tells us to guard it! It affects everything of true value in the human experience!

Jesus Came to Speak to the Heart

In the introduction I defined the heart, for the purposes of this book, as a combination of the mind, will, and emotions. In order to understand that sequence, and to better understand how I am using that word in this book, place three items in a line, in your mind: an ear, a brain, and a heart (not a physical, blood pumping heart, obviously, but the heart as mentioned in the list of scriptures).

Understand that it is a definite possibility for someone to hear something and never have it get to his brain. Just think of any Sunday afternoon during football season. Many a wife asks the husband to do something in the middle of an important part of the game. He hears her audibly but all of his attention is focused on the game. He may even send back a grunt of some sort, but her request never really got to his brain, at least not at a level that understood and considered her comment or request. That communication got to the ear, but not to the brain or to the heart.

Now, think about coming into a movie during its last ten minutes. The movie is a very dramatic movie with deep character development and a powerful plot with many twists and turns. As you slip into your seat you hear the main character say, "but you have no idea how much I love you!" You may see people around you being impacted by that statement, but it doesn't really mean anything to you because you just sat down and don't understand the complex context that has been developed. That communication got through the ear, to the brain, but not to the heart.

Now imagine yourself in a doctor's office, sitting next to your wife. Your doctor has done extensive tests on your child because of a concern for cancer. You have agonized during the wait these past several days. You haven't been able to focus on work or anything else since you first heard about the doctor's concern. The doctor pulls some paper work out of a manila envelope and then mouths the words, "I'm afraid your son has cancer." Everything inside of you is torn apart and your world comes crashing in. Your head spins and you feel your eyes well up with tears as you search in your wife's eyes for help. This communication obviously went through the ear and the brain and reached the heart.

Now, put those three levels of communication into a church setting during a sermon. Can you see the guy staring out the window and thinking about his activities planned for the afternoon? The sermon gets to the ears, but never to the brain. Can you see the guy hearing the words clearly, but so full of arrogance that he could never allow a message of personal guilt and/or repentance to get anywhere near his heart; to the brain, sure, but never to the heart. He understood the pastor's words but was not open to have them be about him. Lastly, can you see the man who hears the message with his heart wide to anything God wants to show him?

My point with this little experiment was not to paint an exact picture of what those three levels of communication look like on people. You never know what it will look like on different people. But I wanted to clearly show that they absolutely do occur in every human being every single day. And speaking through the ear, through the brain, and to the heart is what Jesus was all about.

Jesus, the Great Teacher

If you take even a casual glance at the New Testament, you might question Jesus' ability to convey information. Someone would ask him a question and He would say, "The kingdom of heaven is *like* a pearl" or *like* a number of other things. Can we conclude that if Jesus wanted to speak solely to the brain, then He was a rather poor communicator? People were constantly confused about what He meant by what He said.

If we can agree that Jesus was the smartest person to ever walk the earth then we have to conclude that Jesus' primary goal was *not* simply to get information into their brain, but rather through the brain and all the way into the heart. What was He up to?

Jesus used stories and parables to convey His message. What can stories and parables do that facts and figures cannot do? They can speak much more effectively to the heart. Whenever a preacher is in the middle of a dry sermon and he moves from giving information to telling a story don't you find yourself "waking up" so to speak, and paying closer attention? It is because the stories speak to the heart, where you do your deepest thinking and feeling. That was Jesus' intent.

A few years ago I read a story of a handicapped kid who got to play baseball with the neighbor kids. When the handicapped boy actually connected the bat and the ball, and it dribbled into the infield, in love, the boys faked errors to let him have a home run instead of a simple out at first base. Each time I read the story, it brings me to tears. Why? Because stories can touch you, and move you, and encourage you at a level that information alone cannot. Stories move through the brain and continue on to the heart. In the first five chapters of his book, *Waking the Dead*, John Eldredge does a great job of highlighting and expanding this point.

Recognize and Find Your Heart

- when your child falls and hurts himself, and you are immediately drawn toward him to hold him, that's your heart.

- when you were young and you broke up with your first love, and your insides ached for weeks, that was your heart.

- when the good guy/girl wins in the end of the movie, and something stirs deep inside of you, that's your heart.

- when a song takes you back in time and you find yourself humming along and daydreaming about years gone by, that's your heart.

The heart (mind, will, and emotions) is where Jesus wanted to touch His listeners. And that's where God wants to touch us today. In fact, the heart is where God does the bulk of His work. The heart is what we accept Him into when we become Christians and the heart is where the Holy Spirit resides from that point on. Again, listen to Solomon, "the heart is the wellspring of life." Is that starting to make more sense?

Our Enemy Knows the Value of the Heart

Our enemy knows how valuable the heart is. Satan's ploy is simple, destroy or injure the heart and its ability to love and to be courageous. Doesn't it make sense that Satan would attack our heart? And how does he do that? By putting our hearts in an environment where our hearts get hurt and broken. He is the prince of the power of the air, the prince of this world! He has successfully shaped an environment where we, almost without thinking, pull back from the pain that comes along with having our heart open to people. That's what I did. I still remember the words I told myself, "No girl is ever going to hurt me again."

I am not sure how much credit to give Satan for a harsh and cruel world, but if we go back to Genesis, chapter three, we can give him a large amount of the credit. The reality is that the world is a harsh place, and most men withdraw their heart from loving and caring with abandon. And most of them leave it there.

We must be aware of what is actually happening in the spiritual realm, where Satan is planning and strategizing. We don't consciously choose to make these shifts in our heart, but rather, subconsciously. Much the same way we learn not to touch a hot stove. We don't decide each time to *not* touch the hot stove. Once we learn from our experience, then that knowledge becomes subconscious and we act on it without thinking. We just learn not to do it from experiencing the pain of doing it. And our hearts learn the same way.

I saw these words on a bumper sticker just the other day: "Work as if you didn't need the money, dance as if no one were watching, and love as if you'd never been hurt."

I wish it were possible, but our heart learned to protect itself through fallen parents (*you'll never amount to anything*), fallen first loves (*I don't know what I ever saw in you, I hate you!*), fallen siblings (*I'm gonna tell everyone you wet the bed*), and fallen classmates (*hey, look at four-eyes Petersohn*). Remember, we have not been given a spirit of fear but we have learned it. That's what I did. Maybe that's what you did.

Do you have a wall around your heart? Let me ask you this simple question. Is the full range of your healthy emotions available for those you love? Do you cry when you discuss sad things, hard things? Do you laugh freely when it is called for? Do you easily have fun with those close to you? Is anger reserved for an injustice or does it replace hurt or embarrassment in the blink of an eye. Does frustration quickly rush in to replace and conceal sadness or disappointment? Perhaps more is going on here than just an individual with a certain "style" or personality.

But Jesus said Himself (and I hope it makes a bit more sense to you now) that He came to "heal the brokenhearted." He wants to heal your heart, allowing you to love the Father with *all* of it. If your walk with God has been dry and uneventful, perhaps it is because your heart is unable to fully enjoy and experience God.

Most of us have heard sermons about bearing fruit. We heard about how if we simply abide in the vine, bearing fruit will be a natural thing. I don't know about you but those sermons always frustrated me. Most of my Christian life I felt like I had to work harder to become a better person, to have good things happen to me, and to have good things come out of me.

And now I think I understand why I was frustrated: a person with a broken heart, a walled-off heart, simply cannot abide. You abide with your *heart*. Why do you think most Christians come to salvation before the age of 18? Their hearts aren't shut down.

Can You Relate?

Perhaps you are like me, and you need healing. Perhaps life has laid into your heart and you pulled back because it hurt too much and you wanted the hurting to stop. It sure made sense to me at the time. But it cost me my ability to relate and function in a healthy way with those closest to me.

Do you struggle expressing your healthy emotions to your loved ones? Are you beginning to recognize childhood and teenage experiences that hurt you deeply? Are you starting to recognize some decisions you have made to protect yourself from future hurt, to stop loving with abandon? Are you starting to see some of the individual bricks in the wall around your heart?

In 1 Samuel 10, Samuel takes a flask of oil and pours it over Saul's head. Samuel tells Saul in verse 6 that the Spirit of the Lord was going to come on him and that he would be changed into a different person. In verse 9 Saul actually becomes that different person and it is described in the New Living Translation as God changing Saul's heart. I am ready for a piece of that action, how about you?

Discussion Questions for Chapter 2

What comes to your mind when the subject of the heart is brought up? Is it positive or negative? Is it vague or specific?

What were some of your thoughts as you read through the list of Scriptures? Can you think of any parts of life that do not flow out of the heart? Did your view of the heart change at all from reading the list? If so, in what ways?

Can you list a few things in life that give your heart a lift? Can you list a few things that bring your heart down? On a day-by-day basis, is your heart encouraged or discouraged?

Chapter 3

The Heart of My Problem

*This is my story of recognizing my broken heart
and beginning to realize the connection between it
and my struggles with God and my wife.*

Some truths in the Bible you have to go dig for. Some are sitting right there on the surface, plain as day. One of those clear statements for everyone to see and understand is 2 Timothy 1:7, which tells us that we have not been given a spirit of fear. Plain as day, we have not been given a spirit of fear, but of power, love, and self-discipline. But we have absolutely developed a spirit of fear because life and love are both hard. And, the simplest way to handle painful feelings is to quit feeling so much, to quit caring so much.

The reason many of us don't have a true desire to care about and serve our spouses, is because we decided, a long time ago, out of fear, to quit caring about other people. We *learned* a spirit of fear. We *learned* a spirit of playing it safe, of protecting ourselves from hurting. And in the process, we lost the ability to care about much at all. That's what I did. I lost the ability to feel anything. And while that seems safe, I also lost the ability to truly enjoy life.

The marriage you have always wanted goes down the road of recovering your ability to feel things. It does not go down the road of power or money. It does not go down the road of good looks. To get your feelings back, you need your heart back. To begin to get your heart back, you need to take a look into your past and find out where it got broken, or stolen. This is *my* story of looking back and beginning to heal my heart and my marriage.

My Story

I was born in 1958 in Renton, Washington. I had three older sisters and a younger brother. From what I remember, he and I fought most of the time.

I don't remember having any conversations of substance with either my mom or dad. I'm not really complaining, but stating facts as my memory and perspective allow. Dad taught me how to catch a football without falling down, how to shoot a basketball, and how to pound in a nail, but I don't remember having any heart-to-heart talks with him. I do remember him being a very angry person.

Mom seemed distracted. By the time I was nine she knew she was going to die of an infection in her liver that doctors couldn't cure. But she didn't let on. She just kept trying to keep peace in the family. That seemed to be her job.

Mom took us to church. I became a Christian at a very young age and did all of the right things. I sang solos as a child. I didn't do any "big" sins in my teenage years. I even started directing the church choir at 17. After graduating from high school in 1976, I completed a few years of Navigator Discipleship studies. I was the golden boy.

On November 11, 1979, my mom went into the hospital for the last time. The doctors told us that she wasn't coming home this time. After hearing the news, I drove up to Canada to see my girlfriend. I was scared and didn't know what else to do. I remember crying all the way. I remember picking up a hitchhiker in Marysville and telling him the story about my mom. I remember trying to drown my sorrow by making out with my girlfriend. I remember thinking I was some sort of pervert who'd rather hide in Canada and make out with his girlfriend rather than go home and deal with his mom dying.

When I did get home a few days later, mom was in a coma and died the next day. I remember thinking that mom's last thought about me was probably disappointment because I wasn't there to be with her. I don't remember what I felt other than scared and empty.

After the relationship in Canada ended, I began a relationship with the daughter of my mom's good friend. She was a beautiful girl, and I felt what I believed to be love for the first time. I felt strong and important when I was with her. Her beauty validated who I was as a man. She was my way out. I would be the powerful guy next to the beautiful girl. The guy every other guy wanted to be.

She broke up with me 6 months later and tore my world in two. Then, in the following nine months, she called me up between boyfriends, to hang out. Each time I believed we were back together forever and my problems were solved again. Each break up hurt more and more until I finally told her to never call me again. I felt like I was pushing the lifeboat away from me as I drowned in loneliness. I decided right then and there that no girl was ever going to hurt me again. It didn't seem worth it.

As my emotional world was crumbling, I made an attempt at singing for a living. I made two albums with songs I had written, and for about 4 years I traveled in my car and did small concerts, earning enough money to barely pay the bills. But the adventure, the independence, the freedom, the traveling . . . it was a wonderful time.

When I realized that I wasn't going to be able to make a living doing concerts, I started attending Multnomah School of the Bible and 4 years later came out with a degree in Bible and Youth Ministry. I started my first full-time work as the youth and music pastor at the Enumclaw Evangelical Free Church (later renamed The Summit) in May of 1988.

That same weekend I met Sue. She was beautiful, athletic, and had a warm, natural smile. We started dating, fell in love, and were married two years later.

Carly was born 3 years later. Wow, talk about changes. Kyle was born 2 years later and soon after that Carly was diagnosed with autism. It was hard to hear, but honestly, Carly looked and acted so normal that I believed it was something that would eventually go away. And when Troy was born a few years later, in 1997, I thought we had the perfect family.

I can't say why but the following 3 years brought some introspective thought. Perhaps I was at a place in my life, in my late 30s, where I had done everything I was "supposed" to do. I was a Christian and went to church. I was even a pastor and enjoyed my job. I married a wonderful woman and had three beautiful and wonderful children. The questions in the back of my mind were, "When is this going to start paying off?" and "When am I going to start experiencing the things that God says He came to give me?"

The reality was, while doing and having all the right things, I was empty.

The big shift in my head and my heart started during a pastors' retreat in the spring of 1999. The speaker was trying to convince us that God's individual and personal relationship with us was like a great adventure. I wanted to believe it was true, but I couldn't bring myself to cross that line. God and I ended up in an argument. It was the first *true* argument that He and I had ever had. It was the first time I had been brutally honest with myself or with Him. I told Him that I was sick and tired of pretending that He was strong and powerful. I could no longer ignore my emptiness. Almost 40 years of frustration and confusion came spewing out. It felt good, but scary.

My conclusion was this: I still believed in God, but I was sick and tired of always trying to measure up to what I thought I was supposed to be as a Christian. I was totally fed up with trying to be *good* enough and *disciplined* enough to please Him enough to turn on some "God blessings" that would make me feel good about who I was and what I was doing.

In my frustration I decided to give myself a break. I was going to quit struggling to have daily devotions. And second, I was going to quit beating myself up for not having devotions. I was going to test God a bit and see if He really did love me unconditionally.

My closing statement to Him went something like this: "I still believe in You, but I am done trying to make this God-thing work by doing what everyone else tells me to do." I told God, "I will do whatever You tell me to do, but You have to tell me Yourself!"

And with that, my experiment began. As I remember it, I went a few months without devotions. And every time that I started to berate myself, I reminded myself of my decision, and I allowed myself to not feel bad. Each time I reminded myself that God loved me whether I did my devotions or not.

Then a very special day came. I remember thinking about reading in Ephesians, and as I reminded myself that I didn't *have* to do it, I heard God speak in my heart. He led me to a very specific set of verses, Ephesians 3:16-5:28. It made sense to me that God would lead me there because it included a key set of verses that spoke about marriage, and I knew my marriage wasn't what I had hoped it would be. But I could feel myself starting to fear the discipline needed to make this happen. And almost as I was about to let myself off the hook again God spoke as clearly as I have ever heard Him. He said, "Let's make this about actually changing your marriage. Not about filling some quota for time in the Word."

A light bulb came on. It made sense to me. What God Himself was proposing to me, was that I begin to spend some time in Ephesians, and to make the goal of that time together actual change in my relationship with my wife. What an interesting concept.

My conversation with God went something like this:

"What if I don't feeling like reading one day?"
"Fine."

What if I go a week and don't read anything at all?"
"Fine."
"Should I do inductive study? Should I memorize, or meditate?"
"Let's just spend some time together in My Word."
"Cool. Where? When?"
"What sounds like fun to you?"
"How about up at the river?"
"Sweet. Sounds good."
"Do you mind if I bring my iPod and some worship music?"
"If you'd like to."
"I'm still not sure where this is all going?"
"Just show up and look for me there."
"Okay."

For the next two-and-half years, whenever it felt right to do so, I read portions of Eph 3:16-5:28. I essentially threw out everything Navigators and Multnomah taught me about personal devotions. I started over as a novice, a child. I would simply read until I noticed something that I wasn't doing very well, and tell God with as much honesty as I had at the moment that I wanted to be better at whatever it instructed me to do.

I remember one day up at the river, I was reading Ephesians 4:2 where it says, "make allowance for one another's faults," and I realized I don't do that for Sue. All I could find the strength to say was, "I am *terrible* at this. I *never* make allowance for my wife's faults. God, I don't want to be that way with her. Please help me."

Please catch this picture. A Bible school graduate, tossing out all of his discipleship training and simply sitting by a river and acknowledging his flaws and his desires before God. I remember beginning to feel God again. I remember the simplicity of those times. There were no formulas, no deadlines, no blanks to fill in, and no preset requirements. I just enjoyed opportunities to be honest with Him about what I was doing and how I was feeling.

A Lesson From God

Somewhere during that time in Ephesians, God and I had an encounter that changed my life. Sue and I had just had a big fight, which was not a rare occurrence. We had gone to bed mad, which eliminates me from ever speaking at a marriage conference. We were back to back on our own sides of the bed. We had been in bed about an hour and I believe she was asleep, but I was not. I was furious and angry.

But God started butting in. And what He had to say drove me crazy. He wanted me to roll over and put my arm around Sue. He was ridiculous. Hadn't He seen how she treated me? He heard her words! He obviously knew I was in the right! Why should I be the one to apologize?

He didn't buy my arguments and persisted with His instructions. So I did what I had to do. I rolled over and put my arm around Sue. I even remember saying as I rolled over, "God, I'm only doing this because You told me to do it. Not because I care about Sue at all right now."

As I put my arm around her, she didn't budge. I concluded that she was asleep. But then God showed up. He proceeded to fill me in a way that I hadn't felt in a long time. I felt joy and elation that I simply can't explain. After about 3 or 4 minutes the experience subsided, and I rolled back over to my side of the bed. As I lay there recuperating in amazement, I asked God what that was all about. The answer was simple. He said that that was the kind of fulfillment and joy and satisfaction that *He* was about. That was a hint of how He defined the "fullness of life and power" I had read about in Ephesians 3:19.

I had been a bachelor a long time, and I thought for sure that sex was the answer to fullness of life. This encounter with God was a wakeup call to me on His ability to truly bring joy to my life. No, I didn't take that as a promise that every time I needed Him, He would take me into a trance-like embrace and make me feel incredible. I did sense, though, God showing me that He desired and was able to take me to the deepest levels of who I was, no matter what I was doing.

"You Don't Know How to Be a Friend"

At one point in my journey a coworker at church told me that she thought that I didn't know how to be a friend. I shrugged it off believing that everyone liked me and that I was a nice guy. She told me this during the time I was working my way through Ephesians, wanting to improve my relationship with my wife. In thinking through her statement more, I discovered that I really didn't have any feelings for anyone. This shocked me. I was committed to my wife and to our marriage and to my job, but feelings for people seemed non-existent. My coworker had been correct. I didn't know how to be a friend because I didn't know how to care about anyone but myself. This scared me a bit but intrigued me much more.

You see, several years earlier, our senior pastor had taken the staff on a retreat where we had looked at our past and how it had effected us in both positive and negative ways. It was my first glimpse into the possibility that my past had impacted me in a negative way and might still be controlling me somewhat today. At that time I had no context for those ideas, so they were left unattended. But now, within a context of wanting to fix my marriage and finding my feelings again, these ideas took root and off we went.

The only directions I knew to go were counseling, reading, and talking. It was right about then that another friend tossed a John Eldredge book on my desk, a book I didn't have time to read. But, I ended up reading *The Journey of Desire* three or four times that year. His writing made sense to me and helped me understand more about my heart and its battle to feel.

Talking to people I trusted about the real issues in my life became a staple part of my diet. When people would ask how I was doing, I would stop to pause and think, and then I would really tell them. This tested many a friendship. But each time I did this I was letting God know that I cared more about fixing my problems than I did about looking like I had it all together. And things started changing.

A Growing Awareness of the Issues

I started becoming aware of two realities that called for my attention. The first was that I had made a decision to quit feeling the pain of life. I had moved away from being available to feel. The second thing was an awareness of God's desire to get involved with my heart and not just my mind. I began to see that over-spiritualizing Jesus' desire to heal the broken heart was wrong. I began to see the connection between (1) having a broken heart and (2) being unable to love God. It made sense to me that masking my broken heart would make it impossible to love God with all of it.

Connecting the two dots meant making a decision to work on healing my heart. I decided that there was no greater call on a man's life than to join hands with Jesus and to mend the broken pieces of his heart, in order to love and abide with the Father, and to bear much fruit. And I truly hoped that "much fruit" included a marriage that was exciting and satisfying.

So that is what I did. I began to get some counseling. I dove into books on understanding the heart. I began to tell everyone who would listen about my struggles and dysfunctions. This became my focus, to understand the heart and its function in my world. I desperately wanted to understand how mine was broken, and how being broken held me back from experiencing and enjoying life and love.

Discussion Questions for Chapter 3

How much of what life has to offer are you enjoying? Half? One-tenth? Two-thirds? Restate 2 Timothy 1:7 in your own words. What connection, if any, do you see between enjoying life and being courageous?

What was your reaction to my story? Did you find yourself drawn in, or did you find yourself rejecting me as a man? Why? What parts, if any, of your own story came to mind?

What are your thoughts or concerns about healing the heart? What are your thoughts about focusing on your own heart?

PART TWO: THE FIX

Chapter 4

A Brutal Honesty

*Every time you came home from school late
(pretending to be at swimming practice)
you were lying to us.*
Mary Tyler Moore in "Ordinary People" 1976

Every six months or so I find myself in a very difficult situation. I am sitting in the dentist chair and I am asked a very simple question, "So, how is the flossing going?"

I know what he is asking. He is asking if I am flossing every day. And yet this simple question plays games with my head. I find myself wanting to lie, to put the truth out there in such a way that it passes for acceptable though it is far from the truth. My answer usually goes like this, "not as consistent as I'd like, but it's getting better." That's the coward's way of conveying the truth that I floss about once every month or so.

A brutal honesty is the first critical step in bringing actual change to our lives and to our marriages. If you cannot be honest about your struggles with yourself and with a few others, this journey is over.

If you are like me, this thought puts a knife to your throat. But please understand that I am not saying that every time you sin you need to call someone and confess it. That is not what I am saying. I am saying that you need to be willing to confess every *area* of sin, every tendency to sin, and every dysfunction, to someone.

Did you catch the difference? The dentist in the illustration above wasn't asking me to call him each time I didn't floss. He was asking me to be completely honest with him each time he asked the dreaded question.

Anything Else is Hiding

This brutal honesty needs to be with someone besides God. You and I both know that if the only person we talk to about our struggles is God, we are essentially hiding.

I have concluded that this process of sharing openly with another individual is the clearest definition of obeying God's call to humble ourselves. It seems to me that when we finally confess our sin to someone else we are actually, for the first time, letting God know that we truly want it healed. And that we finally want it healed more than we want to protect our image. And what does He promise? (Go ahead and sing the song to yourself till you find the answer. Humble thyself in the sight of the Lord, and ...) Exactly! He will lift you up. He will lift you up, toward Him, toward healing, toward health, and toward the next step in your growth. This is perhaps the most practical aspect of Solomon's claim that two can do what one cannot (Ecclesiastes 3:4).

Consistency is Key

Another key to a brutal honesty is consistency. Again, I don't mean that you are calling up your accountability partner every 35 minutes and telling him your latest sin. I am saying that in *every* opportunity you have to talk with anyone you trust, at *any* level, you tell the truth, the whole truth, at *that* level of trust.

This concept can be seen clearly in the question that everyone seems to ask everyone else, "how are you doing?" Today's social norm is to simply say without thinking, "everything's fine" or even more simply, "fine." Every time you say things are fine when they are not, you are violating the concept of brutal honesty. True, there are times when you will be asked that question by someone you do not trust at all, and "fine" is the correct answer, but let me give you some suggestions for answers that might be more honest with individuals you trust at a *minimum* level. Let's give this a try...

"How are you doing?"

- "working on some great things"
- "learning to be real honest with myself"
- "wrestling with some crucial issues"

In the same way that an alcoholic seeks to have NO alcohol for fear of slipping off the wagon, a person who hides the truth, as a rule, needs to share the truth every time he has a chance to do so. To hide the truth in a conversation, simply out of fear, is a step backward.

True, there are many people that you will not be comfortable sharing this information with, but I have found that with everyone I feel *some* trust with, I can share *some* truth. Again, when someone I don't know asks me how I am doing, the correct answer is probably, "fine." When someone I trust asks me how I am doing, "fine" would be a copout.

As I share with different people, I have this picture in my mind. I imagine that my fear or my dysfunction is a big barrel full of water. Every time I have an honest conversation about my struggles, both my successes and my failures, I picture taking a small cup of water out of the barrel and tossing it onto a hot sidewalk, letting the sun evaporate it quickly. With each cup of water removed do I see a difference in the water level in the barrel? No, but over time I know that the water level will begin to show change, with the barrel eventually being empty.

That is the power of many quality conversations over a substantial time period. When James 5:16 tells us that confessing our faults to one another brings healing, it doesn't say it will happen immediately. There is no time frame on it. I believe that reality demonstrates that this is usually accomplished over a substantial period of time.

This brutal honesty does demand, though, a good amount of wisdom. Telling the wrong person the wrong thing could be a major distraction or setback in your healing. If your porn problem surfaced at church it could have serious repercussions. If your lust issues were to surface at work, things could get very awkward and difficult. You get my point.

There are two things to remember here. First, I have already mentioned the need to tell the appropriate amount of information to the individual based on how much you can trust him.

Second, the primary issues that I am addressing in this book are not about individual sins or habits, but the dysfunctions that lie underneath those sins. Imagine speaking to a small group of men at your church. Imagine the different impact between saying, "I struggle with lust" versus telling them which woman in the church you are currently lusting after. Being as wise as foxes means being careful *how* your share the information you decide to share.

The Value of Transparency

My favorite movie of all-time is "Good Will Hunting." Will is a hardened young man who was raised in the foster-care system. As a youth he was physically abused in horrible ways. He is befriended by his counselor and begins to trust him. Toward the end of the movie, his counselor repeatedly reminds him that the abuse was not his fault. With the repeated reminder, Will is slowly broken down to the point of crying and hugging his counselor, honestly showing for the first time, some of the pain the abuse inflicted.

Many people, mostly men, struggle with my view of crying. Though it doesn't prove anything, I believe crying is often an indicator of some level of transparency. And I even go so far as to say that an inability to cry is often an indicator that full transparency is not happening. You can decide for yourself on that one.

My point is this, until we are truly transparent, until we completely revisit the injury, until we are loved in that moment by someone we trust, we will not find healing. To revisit the injury and find acceptance rather than injury, allows the heart to begin or continue its journey of health and growth. Watch the movie for yourself (it is rated R for language). Notice the very valid and insightful connection between the transparency and the subsequent healing. This is crucial to understand.

If someone else injured us, we must be honest about the pain it caused us. If we sinned and brought injury to others and ourselves, we must be honest about our blame. Skirt this concept and healing will totally elude us.

I was writing one morning in a local coffee shop and watching a friend of mine sitting and chatting with her daughter. I'd seen them there often. My friend's ex-husband was not a good husband or father. He cheated on her and abandoned the family. As I watched them, I did not know what they were talking about, but I do know that those conversations were giving the daughter a better chance at having a healthy marriage someday. Those conversations were gently and slowly healing some of the damage that the divorce inflicted. Oh, the power of a quality conversation with someone you trust.

Let's look at some areas of honesty that I have found very helpful.

Honesty About Our Disappointment With God

I lived the "perfect" Christian life and yet at the end of 40 years of doing all the right things I still had to cover for God because nothing ever truly satisfied me and nothing, absolutely nothing, ever changed. We can, and need to be honest about this.

It's true that it is never God's fault if we are not changing or are not satisfied. He is 100% for positive change and growth in us. The point of the honesty is not to blame God, but to start being honest about how we feel and where we struggle in our experience with God. And most of us have areas of significant spiritual disappointment that we need to be honest about.

The couple that never fights is not necessarily showing a level of health. Look again at King David. He was often angry or frustrated at God, and God never held it against him. In fact it was a positive part of their relationship, and it demonstrated David's health, not his dysfunction.

Honesty About the Damage Life Has Inflicted on Us

A brutal honesty insists that we take a close look at our childhood, our parents and siblings, and our early love experiences.

My dad was a pretty angry guy. That's what I remember most. I don't remember having any heartfelt conversations with him. Mom was juggling an angry husband, five children, and the knowledge that she was going to die soon. I don't remember having any quality conversations with her either. The problem with that is that moms and dads are supposed to help prepare kids for being adults. I don't remember that happening in my home. I'm not trying to blame them; I'm simply recognizing the beginning of a problem.

After my mom passed away in 1979, I started dating someone, hoping she would ease the pain in my heart. When she broke up with me the following year, I determined that no girl was ever going to hurt me again. Is it any wonder I struggled having feelings for anyone?

What's your story? Are you willing to talk about it, to face it? My point is not that you have to be willing to confront the one who hurt you but simply to discuss it with someone you trust, openly and honestly. In all of my journeys into my past, I never heard God telling me I had to confront any of those that disappointed me. He simply wanted to stand beside me as I faced it, to weep over it with me, and to begin to heal me.

We all have stories of encounters with fallen humans. Close family members and complete strangers all fall into the category of fallen and sinful, and they are all capable of inflicting harm on us, intentionally or unintentionally. We all have stories. Where or how has life damaged your heart? We need to talk and be brutally honest about these stories.

Honesty About Our Fears

Do you know why so many men struggle with anger? Because they feel embarrassed and are afraid of looking weak and wrong. Do you know why men are usually passive when it comes to initiating sex with their wives? They are afraid of the response that they are used to getting. I am not saying that those wives are not at some level of fault in the issue, but the reality of it is that men are afraid of rejection. Do you know why most men rarely show any tender emotions? They are afraid of being seen as weak.

I am getting convinced that most men are ruled by fear. And yet 2 Timothy 1:7 tells us that the spirit of fear is not from God. We are fearful, but it never fits us. We have learned it from life, but it will never fit us.

What are you afraid of? In this situation it might be a significant first step to simply start being honest with *yourself* about these areas. Very few of us take the time to investigate the possibility of fear in our heart. But to do this is crucial. If we want to build courage into our lives, we have to face our enemy. We have to know him by name. What are you afraid of? Can you be honest here?

Honesty About Our Arrogance

Romans 12:3 instructs us to not see ourselves as more valuable than we are. Not all, but a good portion of the men I have deeper conversations with struggle with this. Many struggle deep in their heart, where no one but God sees, with a belief that they are smarter and more capable than their wives. They see themselves as more valuable to the relationship than their wives. Somewhere in the creases of their heart they see the helpmate role as subservient.

Perhaps you need to look into that Old Testament term found in Genesis 2:18. The Hebrew word for "helper" or "helpmate" is used in only two other places in the Old Testament. In both of those instances they refer to God Himself, and the role He plays in each instance is that of a warrior and a lifesaver. In other words, if God doesn't come to the rescue, someone is dying.

Does that make it sound like the helpmate is less important in the relationship? I understand that much old- school thinking puts women in a less-than role, but that needs to stop now if you want to move forward from here. The role of headship, given to the man, is there because of gifting, not because of value. The Bible could not be clearer here. The marriage begins with mutual submission to one another (Ephesians 5:21). In Christ all are equal (Colossians 3:11).

Are we willing to admit this attitude is sinful and unbiblical? Are we willing to admit this is cowardice at its finest? Do you have the honesty to admit this sin and begin to see your wife's value? Are you man enough for that?

Honesty About the Idols in Our Lives

Yes, we all sin, and we obviously need to address the issues of individual sin in our lives. But underneath those individual sins, can you be honest about the idols in your life that lead you to the doorstep of sin? Yes, lust is a sin. Yes, we should confess it and deal with it when it happens. But the reason most men end up lusting is because sex is an idol for them. They bow before the altar of sex, seeing its value incorrectly.

Does sex control your behavior when you are around your wife? When you are around other women? When you are on your computer and no one is looking?

Is money your idol? Does your desire for money drive you to work too long or to worry about not having enough?

Are you worshiping control? Do you want control in situations where you don't have it? Does a lack of control make you stressful or angry?

And can you admit it? Not in a, "yeah, so what? Everybody thinks that way!" way. But in a, "Yeah, I really do, and I wish I didn't" way. (Think back to the flossing question.)

The good news is that being able to ask yourself these questions, and to think through and admit the answers, is actually the beginning of the solution to the problem. You may be thinking to yourself that having idols eliminates you from moving forward with God, and I say wrong! *Hiding* your idols eliminates you from moving forward. Remember that admitting to someone else that you have these idols is saying to God, perhaps for the first time, that you want them gone!

See the difference? It is huge! One ignores God, His word, and is hiding and cowardice. The other is courageous and humbling, and a great first step toward getting some real help.

Discussion Questions for Chapter 4

What do you most often talk about with your friends? How deep do you go in conversations with your best friends? What is your reaction to the idea of "going deep" in conversations? Why?

Have you ever been disappointed with God? What were the circumstances? What did you do with your disappointment? How did the disappointment resolve itself? If it has not completely been resolved, is there any residue in your heart from the disappointment?

Think back to your story and describe your childhood. What is your favorite memory? What did you learn from it? What memory would you most like to forget but cannot? What can you learn from it?

Chapter 5

A Barbaric Courage

Courage is not shown by the strength to do anything,
or to do everything.
Courage is demonstrated by the strength to do
the next thing.

This is my command – be strong and courageous!
Do not be afraid or discouraged.
For the Lord your God is with you wherever you go.
Joshua 1:9

Perhaps the most crucial thing you need to understand in developing a barbaric courage in your life is that the courage to get started begins to grow when you start developing a brutal honesty, as described in the previous chapter. God is not going to give you the second step toward courage if you have skipped the first step out of fear.

My experience is this; when you take that first step of being brutally honest with another person, God will lift you up so that you can see the next step and have the courage to take that step.

So feel free to read through this whole book and to consider being more courageous in your life, but don't expect courage to start developing while you are allowing fear to rule over you, keeping you from telling other people about your fear. Makes sense, right?

Paper Tiger

We must begin here by understanding that your fears are not necessarily something worth fearing. What I mean is this; to be fearful of your child playing on the freeway during rush hour traffic is a very real and worthwhile fear. They could actually get hurt or killed. That is a good and appropriate fear. However, to be afraid to pray with your wife is not a good or appropriate fear.

- To be afraid of being the first to say you're sorry after a fight is a paper tiger.

- To be afraid of considering the fact that you may have a sexual addiction problem is a paper tiger.

These are not fears that could result in physical harm. What could these fears result in? Embarrassment, it seems to me, is the issue.

We need to see this fear of embarrassment as the paper tiger that it is. A paper tiger is something that looks dangerous on the outside, but ultimately has no power to truly harm you.

- The fear of staying after church and actually starting a conversation with someone is a paper tiger.

- The fear of starting to attend a small group at your church is a paper tiger.

- The fear of developing a relationship with someone to the point of actually trusting them with your struggles is a paper tiger.

- The fear of telling someone you trust that you often lose your temper with your kids is a paper tiger.

Are you beginning to see how these hidden fears rule and run our lives much of the time?

- How about your fear to admit true weakness to anyone?

- How about your struggle to look someone in the eye when the conversation gets emotional?

- How about your struggle to share your love for your wife in words that are more than catch-phrases?

- How about your struggle to say "I'm sorry" when you absolutely know you are wrong about something?

- How about your inability to cry about things that *should* break your heart?

- How about your fear to initiate sex with your wife? Not to *ask* for it, or to *demand* it, or to *whine* about not getting it, but Song of Solomon initiating!

- How about your refusal to call a counselor and get some help when you know deep inside you that you have some serious struggles that are breaking your wife's heart?

The good news here is that with every paper tiger that is broken through, you brush up against "fullness of life." And each time you break through a paper tiger, you gain the strength to break through the next one. Every time you follow God's prompting and overcome your fear, you find yourself touched at your core, and it feels very good. As my wife said in a talk she recently gave, this kind of courage brings with it a "strangely refreshing" sensation.

An Example of "Strangely Refreshing"

We were on a date night a few months ago, and I had heard God tell me to ask Sue about the harm I had caused her over the first eighteen years of our marriage. It scared me, but I knew I had to obey, so after dinner I asked her the question. It shocked her at first, and she figured I didn't really want to hear the answer. But I kept pursuing the truth.

After about an hour of checking out my motive, Sue finally broke, and I heard her heart for the first time. In essence she told me the same stuff she had been telling me for the eighteen years prior. But this time, for the first time, she told me with tears in her eyes and with her heart wide open to the hurt it was feeling, and it moved me. Her frustration moved aside and this time the pain in her heart told the story. For the first time I actually *heard* her. For the first time I was able to truly apologize. And for the first time I actually yearned to fix my behavior.

I gained all of that by breaking through *my* paper tiger and asking the question. Sue really helped me learn by breaking through *her* paper tiger and revealing her heart and not just her defensiveness. In the weeks since, probably three or four times now, I have come to her with tears in my eyes to lay my head in her lap and to apologize again for the eighteen years of pain I caused her, pain that I didn't see until I heard her heart. Those paper tigers stand between us and some incredible growth and experiences.

Kicking the Can Down the Street

There is a phrase that I use to describe the process of showing a barbaric courage and healing. This phrase is "kicking the can down the street." One key to this phrase focuses on the fact that you can't kick the can a long way down the street and then rest while you walk up to it. Those darn empty cans just won't go that far even if you nail it with a perfect kick. Very soon you have to kick it again. It is a constant and consistent process.

Also, notice that if you miss the can you have to go back and attempt the kick again. If you miss the can, there is not another can a few steps farther down the road waiting for you. You must go back and attempt to kick the original can again. If I say "no" to God's prompting, I miss the can, and things halt until I go back and kick the can. A fear that you are facing needs to be dealt with or the process stops. Until you find the courage to face it, the next step will not present itself. But when you do face that fear, the next one presents itself and you find yourself with a bit more courage to face it. And on down the road toward healing you go.

It needs to be mentioned again that the initial step of building this courage is the honesty mentioned in chapter 4. So many people want to avoid having to talk honestly about their struggles with someone they trust. I know that it is natural for you to want to find a way around that first step. It probably seems like more than you can bear, but it is absolutely necessary. But remember two things. I am not asking you to tell someone about every single sin, but about the area of sin in general. Second, it is this step that first shows God your deepest desire.

Baby Steps

Next, you need to understand that courage is not demonstrated by the strength to do anything, or to do everything. Courage is demonstrated by the strength to do the *next* thing.

Another one of my favorite movies is Bill Murray's "What About Bob?" Bob, who struggles mightily with several mental and emotional disorders, finds the strength to move forward in his mixed up world by dividing the huge complex mess of his world into multiple, consecutive, baby steps. And then he proceeds to take them on one at a time. "Baby step out of the office, baby step into the elevator, baby step out of the elevator, baby step onto the sidewalk, etc…"

Baby Dives

Imagine being afraid of going off of a fifty-foot diving board into a deep pool of water. For many of us that is a very legitimate fear. But can you also imagine starting with a three-foot diving board, doing ten dives a day, and adding an inch to the height of the board every day? You would be jumping off of a fifty-foot board in less than two years. That still may sound scary, but at least it appears feasible, doesn't it!

God used that sort of process, a "baby step" process, to give me the courage I needed to overcome my moodiness. I had a pattern of getting angry at Sue. She would do something that would upset me. I would make her pay for what she did by getting upset and not talking to her in any sort of loving way for a few days. It wasn't so much a decision I made to make her pay for hurting my feelings. It just seemed like it needed to be done in order to discipline her for what she did, to help her see what it did to me and to help her not do it again. (Please hear this as dysfunction, not logic.)

To her, it came across as me being in a bad mood, and it just drove her further away from loving and respecting me.

As God helped me, through talking with others, I came to understand my broken heart and its dysfunctions. It was at this point that I realized that my "moodiness" was a device I had developed to protect myself from the apparent hurt that Sue was inflicting on me. I had developed this pattern because I was too afraid to simply share my feelings with her.

It's important to note here that it didn't matter if Sue actually behaved toward me in an unloving way. That was not the issue. Whether she did or did not act unloving, pulling away from her and making her "pay" was not the correct response. Don't miss the point of this illustration by blaming Sue's behavior. It didn't matter what she was or was not doing. My response must be to own my issues first.

Baby Stepping to Health

As God revealed this moodiness to me and helped me to own it, He began to slice off little bits of challenge and asked me to show little bits of courage. The progression of those little bits of challenge looked something like this:

- At the end of a few days of "making her pay," admitting that I was *probably* wrong for treating her poorly.

- At the end of a few days of "making her pay," admitting that I was wrong for treating her poorly.

- After a day or so admitting I was wrong. (As I remember it took several months to get to this point)

- Apologizing for being wrong as I stormed away at the end of the argument.

- Admitting that I was probably wrong in the middle of the argument.

- Admitting that I was probably wrong at the beginning of the argument. (Probably another several months)

- Wondering if I was seeing things through my dysfunction as I overreacted to what Sue said.

- Wondering if I was seeing things through my dysfunction and softening my overreaction to what Sue said.

- Deciding that I was probably seeing things through my dysfunction and deciding not to say anything though still frustrated with her comment.

- Deciding that I was probably hearing Sue wrong and asking her, with a decently calm tone, about the meaning of what she said.

- Deciding that whether Sue was right or wrong, my overreaction is a bigger issue than whatever she said, and owning the responsibility to calm down before I said anything.

Do I get it right every time? No, but this is about where things are right now. I figure I have about another year or more of work before I simply hear what she is saying from a healthy heart. And when she does say something with a "tone" or hint of accusation, I hope to be able to respond in love as her partner and friend.

During the whole process of beginning to heal my moodiness, I was having conversations with men I trusted about it. Those conversations gave me the courage to take those baby steps. As God used those conversations to heal my heart, it did what a healthy heart was supposed to do, grow courage. It was that courage that I used to step through each paper tiger, slowly tearing away my dysfunction and growing healthy reactions.

Do you see the process? Do you see how God sliced off a bit of the dysfunction each time and asked me to grow and show courage? Do you see how the conversations grew the courage to take the next step? No, I did not always succeed the first time I attempted to be courageous. Neither will you. But remember, when you miss the can, you need to go back and give the kick another attempt. There is no "next can" waiting down the road. You need to go back and pass the test before God will show you your next step of courage.

The Most Difficult Can to Kick

Perhaps the easiest place to "miss the can" is in the beginning moments of an argument. Is seems so difficult, nearly impossible, to consider the possibility that we are seeing things through the eyes of our dysfunction.

The good news is that God believes in baby steps. I know God can heal me completely today. But I also know He probably won't. So what does He expect? He expects me to do something about my dysfunction and sin every day, unpeeling the onion, one layer at a time, with every opportunity I am given. Remember, the courageous man is the man with the courage to do the *next* thing!

What is Really Going On Here?

"Dear brothers and sisters, whenever trouble comes your way, let it be an opportunity for joy. For when your faith is tested your endurance has a chance to grow" (James 1:2-3).

Those verses never truly made sense to me until I had made it my priority to change and to grow. Now I see trials as an opportunity for me to kick the can further down the street. No, I am not happy when I face a trial (often an argument with Sue), but just behind my "not liking it" is an understanding that something else is going on here. I am starting to see that life is not full of coincidences. Life is full of carefully prepared circumstances, many of them trials, to get us to move in the right direction. Every single trial we encounter goes through the hand of God to help us move toward Christ-likeness.

After my mom passed away, we found the following quote from Alan Redpath written on a scrap piece of paper in her Bible.

There is nothing– no circumstance, no trouble, no testing – that can ever touch me until, first of all it has gone past God and past Christ, right through to me. If it has come that far, it has come with a great purpose which I may not understand at the moment. But as I refuse to become panicky – as I lift up my eyes to Him – and as I accept it as coming from the throne of God for some great purpose of blessing to my heart, no sorrow will ever disturb me, no trial will ever disarm me, no circumstance will cause me to fret – for I shall rest in the joy of what my Lord is. That is the rest of victory.

The arguments with our wives are trials that have a purpose. They are not simply indicators that something is wrong, but, more so, they are springboards to conversations that lead to growth. All we need is the courage to risk and respond to the argument differently than we normally do. That may be the most difficult risk ever, but you can do it, and it must be done.

Let's look at this just a bit deeper and see what God might be up to. When we have an argument and feel our wives have treated us poorly, why are they doing that? Is it because they are instinctively mean and devious? No! It is because they are hurting, and in their own weakness and dysfunction they lash out in an attempt to feel better or to protect themselves. We know what that feels like. But this is exactly the time when they need us to love them the most. This is when the prince needs to show up and be brave. It takes a man of courage to respond in love when he feels his wife has attacked him.

When our wives are in an unhealthy place, they desperately need us to come to them gently and love them.

- When we are in the middle of an argument, they need us to be strong and pursue their heart, their hurt, and their fear. They need us to not respond in kind to their attack, which is born out of hurt. Are you man enough for that?

- When you turn your back and walk out on your wife during an argument, in order to punish her, she needs you to turn back around, to say you are sorry, and to reengage with a soft heart. She needs to begin to see you as safe, that you won't abandon her when the times get tough. Are you man enough for that?

- After an argument is over, but before a reconnection is made, she needs you to laugh, to show that you are not holding a grudge. She needs you to want to be reconnected and to pursue that reconnection. She needs you to move toward her physically and to touch her face and tell her that she is beautiful. She needs you to look her in the eyes and tell her that you truly are sorry for your part of the argument. She needs you to cuddle with her in bed without moving toward sex. Are you man enough for that?

- When she calls you on the phone, and just wants to talk, she needs you to pay careful attention. She needs you to understand the value of caring enough to listen. She needs you to ask questions to help her dig deeper into her thoughts and feelings.

She needs you to celebrate her love of, and need for, communication. Are you man enough for that?

Remember, fear never fits us, "For God has not given us a spirit of timidity, but of power and love and self discipline." God's yoke fits us. The challenges above are God's yoke for real men. And we get to choose our yoke. We can choose either the yoke of courage, the yoke that fits us, doing the right but difficult thing. Or we can choose the yoke of cowardice, of failing ourselves, our wives, and God. We get to choose. But fear never fits. Courage always fits.

So when God puts that "next step" in front of you, that next baby step, He is calling you to courage, to something that fits you and will ultimately satisfy you richly and deeply.

Discussion Questions for Chapter 5

Did any of the "paper tigers" examples hit home with you? Which ones? In your own words, how are paper tigers harmless? What are they keeping you from feeling, or experiencing, or knowing?

Why is it easier to focus on your wife's sin rather than your own? Is your wife's sin ever an excuse for your sin? What would it take for you to ignore your wife's sin and completely own the responsibility for your own sin?

In practical terms, describe the satisfaction that God promises us if we do what is right. How does it compare to the satisfaction that comes from winning an argument?

Chapter 6

An Enduring Perseverance

*Growing courage where injury thrives
is one of the greatest battles known to mankind.
Where do we lean when we want to give up?*

-----

*For I can do everything through Christ
who gives me strength.
Philippians 4:13*

In a time-management seminar I attended many years ago, I was taught that every element of our waking day can be divided up into four different categories:

Not important/not urgent (channel surfing, reading the cartoons)
Not important/urgent (The American Idol finals are on tonight!)
Important/urgent (the kids missed their bus, the car needs gas)
Important/not urgent (exercising, dieting)

Please note that the description of "non-urgent" has absolutely nothing to do with its importance or value. It merely reflects the lack of motivation to accomplish the task that the task brings with it.

With that understanding you can see how every spiritual discipline and every important human discipline falls into the "important/non-urgent" category! Exercise, dieting and intellectual study all fail to bring with them daily motivation to accomplish them. All of the greatest challenges of life, including raising kids and growing a great marriage lack the daily motivation to accomplish the tasks by giving the *appearance* that nothing will really change if we wait one more day to get started. But we all know that is not true.

Healing our dysfunction and building a courageous heart obviously fall into that category as well. They take time and effort. But because it falls into the non-urgent category, it does not automatically come with the motivation to accomplish the task. That's why persevering is so difficult. The task has to be placed on the front burner of your mind and attention, and then it has to be held there. Perseverance is key in building the marriage you have always dreamed of. The following are some things that I have learned about finding the strength for the long haul.

Our Daily Manna

Hosea 13:4-6 tells of the nation of Israel crying out to God because of their huge need. After God met the need, they became satisfied and forgot about God. That is what they did, and that is what we do on a regular basis. It is our daily tendency to forget God unless a trial, a clear need for God, is in view.

Larry Crabb reminds us in his book, *The Difference Between Men and Women*, that the differences between men and women are simply daily trials that allow couples to be reminded, every single day, that their spouse was not put there to meet their deepest need. That is God's job. And God provides a daily solution, manna.

The story of the manna in Exodus 16 is a clear picture of what God wants to give us every single day, what we need to survive. Manna, a bread-like substance, which came with the dew every morning, could be gathered every morning and the food would sustain them through their time in the desert, one day at a time. Lamentations 3:23 adds a bit more color with the promise that God's mercies were new *every morning*. This is a clear reference to God's daily provision for His children.

For us, this manna is traditionally labeled as daily devotions. I, myself, don't like the term because it tends to come with such harsh boundaries. The traditional definition is that it *has* to include traditional Bible reading and it *has* to include traditional prayer.

Look at Jesus' example. We are told that He got up early in the morning, to go out into the wilderness, and to spend time with His Father (Mark 1:35). We are also told in Luke 5:16 that these personal escapes into the wilderness were His regular routine. But that is *all* we are told about His "devotions." It seems to me that we are free to ask the simple but important question, "God, what do You want *our* focused time together to look like?"

God Doesn't Shove Us Into a Mold

Solomon, in His God-given wisdom, understood the value of raising children according to their built-in differences. That is the heart of the message of Proverbs 22:6 "Direct your children onto the right path, and when they are older, they will not leave it." This is not a promise that if you raise a kid in the church, and he wanders away from God, that he will ultimately come back to the Lord. A much closer interpretation is that every child is unique, and has a special way about them. This is the way they should go. You don't make a bookworm go an athlete's way. You don't force a tomboy into a ballerina's way. We are instructed to help that child to learn his or her way, the way God has made them unique and wonderful. It makes sense that God would do the same with us as He raises us and spends quality time with us.

I strongly encourage every one of you to take the time to sincerely ask God what *your* daily manna will look and taste like. He wants to create a unique relationship with you and it seems both biblical and logical that He would create it by going down a unique road with you. He doesn't cookie-cut any of His children.

Realistic Expectations

If you are going to persevere, you are going to have to give yourself some room to fail. In my ten years of wrestling with my fears, I have never had a day go by in which I won every match. Most days have been two forward, one back. Or in more realistic terms, 28 forward and 27 back. The task of changing the way we think is an arduous task. Not every time, but most of the time. God may choose to reach in and do a miracle. I've experienced it myself. But most likely God will do the miracle over time, slowly but surely, the same way we developed the wrong thinking.

A Battle Companion

Let's look back for a moment at Solomon's insight into the value of a friend. When he talks about the one helping the other to get up after he has fallen, he is talking about getting back up after a failure and getting back in the game. He says it again when he talks about someone watching your back in battle. And don't tell me battling your dysfunctions isn't a real battle. We have a very real enemy. The Bible is absolutely literal at this point! Don't fool yourself. Twenty eight forward and twenty seven back is a good day, or a good week, but it takes having someone there to help you back up those twenty seven times. Perseverance takes a battle companion. That's all there is to it.

I have a million stories spanning my twenty years of being a pastor where a person will start something good and fade away after a short burst of enthusiasm. (And some of those failures are about me!) Pity the Christian that enters the battle without someone to watch his back. Perseverance is a pipedream without a battle companion. But *with* a battle companion, a barbaric perseverance is possible. Downright tempting, I hope!

Giving it Time

Everyone is different, and there are many factors that will determine how long it will take (how old you are when you start, how many years of the dysfunction settling in, how severe the dysfunction, etc.) but don't expect it to be short or sweet. I do not say this to discourage you but to prepare you. You need to know what you are facing so that you can prepare for the journey. The Gospel of Luke tells us that a smart king decides if he has enough men to win the battle before he enters it. Also, that a smart builder makes sure that he has enough to complete the project to keep from being laughed at. Good advice.

Rejoice, though, in the fact that the very first step will bring with it an inner nudge that will intrigue and point you toward true satisfaction. You will feel a new breeze in the air. You will get a small glimpse of heaven and the joy it offers.

What Women Want

One of the things that truly motivated me to keep going was when I began to understand how attractive being brave is to a woman. They can smell out the difference between courage and arrogance very easily.

A reality show I was watching the other night about celebrities in a rehab program showed a stunning example of this. Gary Busey was injured in a car wreck, suffered some brain damage, and obviously has some mental and emotional struggles resulting from it. His usual behavior appears so haphazard and arrogant that it drives those around him crazy. He thinks he is everyone's answer and tries to fix everyone else.

In a very special scene, he was being unusually honest with the group about his injury and how it makes him act so strange. This is something that he rarely admitted. A woman in the group, in a moment of honesty and insight said, "You have never been more attractive than you are right now." Did you catch that? She began to see him as handsome and beautiful (the opposite of her reactions to him before) when he started being honest about his struggles and about his fears. You need to vividly remember that the princess loves the prince primarily because he is brave, not because he is handsome.

I had always wanted to believe that the princess loved the prince because he desired her often and she loved the attention. It was a very helpful day when I let that notion go. The day I finally put courage at the top of Sue's "most needed and desired" list was a good day. That day did a lot in building a persevering strength in my heart.

Women don't need perfection. They need honesty and some hard work. These are both very respectable qualities. A man who is willing to admit his struggles and begin to work on them is on his way to becoming the prince his princess longs to love.

Guarding Your Heart

The challenge of guarding our heart is a book unto itself, but let's mention a few things here. The obvious first step in guarding your heart is to work toward a healthy heart, as described throughout this book.

For most men then, guarding your heart, protecting your investment, comes down to some fairly simple disciplines. The discipline of getting your daily manna from God would be first. That daily time alone with Him, heart to heart, receiving His daily mercies, is like filling up the fuel tank at the gas station. And it automatically reminds us that our deepest needs are His to meet, not our wives.

Second, I believe that we men need to learn to steer away from many good things that can distract us. Overtime at the office and the night out with the guys are good things. But because they fit us in so many ways they can become distractions to the more difficult things that end up being more crucial to life. Remember, Hebrews 12:1 reminds us to strip off every weight that weighs us down. These are not necessarily sins, but perhaps good things that keep us from the better things.

Third, I think that men need to get more comfortable with time alone or at least time in a quiet setting. People in general tend to lean toward noisy environments because it keeps them from having to feel bored or introspective. But it is most likely in those quiet times that

God and/or our heart will talk to us, and it is in that same quiet place that we will most likely be able to hear them.

Lastly and by no means is this exhaustive, men need to learn to enjoy beauty. Let me be more specific, beauty beyond that of a naked female body. Music, art, and nature are just three of the incredible things that our world offers us to feed and massage our hearts. I know that this sounds very feminine, but we have to get over this ignorance that masquerades as strength or toughness. We are being foolish if we refuse to acknowledge the value of simply enjoying the beautiful things in life at a slow and relaxed pace.

Discussion Questions for Chapter 6

Reread the first page of this chapter and list a few items in your non-urgent/non-important quadrant. List a few items in your urgent/non-important quadrant. List a few in your urgent/important quadrant. Lastly, list all of the items you can think of that go in your non-urgent/important quadrant. Discuss your findings.

Describe your quiet times. Do they "fit" you or do you feel shoved into a mold? What level of satisfaction or excitement do you experience in your relationship with God? What level do you believe is possible? What stands in the way?

Are there any men in your life that know the real you? In general terms, describe what they know and what they don't know. How are those relationships nurtured and/or utilized? Why do you think this level of friendship is so rare?

PART THREE:
THE PROCESS

Chapter 7

Moving Forward Into Actual Change

This is not a trip to the corner grocery store.
This is a trip to the center of your universe.
It will take all of your strength and courage.
Packing poorly will be fatal.

Are you tired of having to make excuses for God not coming through? Are you tired of saying that God is incredible but feeling nothing incredible in your life? Are you tired of seeing absolutely nothing of substance changing in your life? Wouldn't it be fun to see God reach in and actually fix something? Wouldn't it be fun if the change was obvious enough that even those people who love us enough *not* to like us once in awhile could see it!

Most of the people I talk to about God have trouble giving clear examples of how God has changed their lives. Circumstances change, getting older brings natural change, but most people cannot give clear examples of how God has actually changed a bad habit into a discipline, a dysfunction into healthy behavior, or a dysfunctional relationship into a healthy relationship.

Seems a bit odd doesn't it? God is powerful, so we say, and yet He seems impotent to actually change anything substantive. Why is that? And why is it that it doesn't seem to bother us much that things don't change?

I believe that the reason we give up on God's ability to bring change is because we believe that the missing key is a level of spiritual discipline that we just simply cannot attain. And since we could never get there, the only option is to lower our expectations of what God has to offer.

I hope that we are beginning to change that subconscious line of thought. I hope that you are getting convinced that an unhealthy heart has been the real culprit.

My D-Day

It was a beautiful morning and I was excited to get down to the waterfront and spend some time with God. I drove to a favorite spot, plugged in my iPod, pulled out my Bible, and began to plug into God and into what He wanted to show me and tell me that morning. Somewhere in the middle of my time with Him I began to feel excited about being married to Sue.

You've got to understand this moment. Sue and I had been married about fifteen years and were in the middle of raising three kids. Our romance had run the normal course and we were comfortable with each other. We were very committed, but I am not sure either one of us felt in love with each other.

So when God reached down and handed me some "in love" feelings for my wife it was a big deal. And the exciting thing to me was that we had scheduled breakfast together later that morning. I sat there on the waterfront and imagined sharing my excitement with my wife in the restaurant later that morning. It was going to be glorious. She would feel so cared for, and I would feel so strong.

About an hour later, as I sat across from her in the restaurant, I was tongue-tied. I tried everything I could do to get the words and the thoughts out, but I could not do it. I felt locked up inside. I felt hog-tied. I felt broken.

That was my D-Day. That was the last day that I said that I was okay and that everything was fine. I was *not* okay.

I had been looking back at my past and had seen how some events and people had hurt me. I had talked to some counselors and some good friends about my struggles, but that day was different. That day I quit hiding the truth. That day I acknowledged the fact that my heart was not functioning properly, that my heart was unable to be and do what it was built to be and do.

Are you done hiding the truth? Are you man enough to say the heart is crucial to living life? Are you man enough to say that your heart is not running on all eight cylinders? Are you man enough to say that fear holds you back from living life to the full? If you are, then it's time to take a look forward and take back the life, the love, and the marriage that the Evil One robbed from you.

Preparing For the Journey

As we move forward, I want you to imagine a workout session with free weights. (The heart is a muscle, you know!) In order to build muscle we need to break it down a bit, and let it re-grow itself bigger and stronger. That's how lifting weights work. You lift until you can't lift any more. You lift until you, somewhat, "break" the muscle. The muscle, thinking that you are going to demand it to lift that amount of weight again, will rest and heal, and grow itself bigger and stronger in order to do a better job the next time.

As you press on toward actual change, it will feel like you are damaging the heart. It will feel like you have pushed it too far. But what you have done is begun to work the muscle, and it will begin to grow in health and strength. And God will see that you are serious about wanting your heart back. He will see that you are serious enough to actually do something about it, and He will respond.

As you begin this process be sure to notice the interworking of a healing heart and the courage it both demands and grows. As your heart grows healthy, it will automatically grow some courage with it. And it is in pushing yourself past your emotional limits, in crossing that comfort zone line, that you will find your heart healing. It is absolutely a two-way street.

Be ready. You will want to quit. Your unhealthy heart will scream at you that it hurts too much, and that it is going nowhere quickly. You will need to pack very carefully for this journey. The most dangerous journeys demand the most careful packing. The same is true for extended journeys. This journey of discovering and healing your heart is both dangerous and extended.

A Lesson Learned

A few years ago, on a trip to Hawaii with the family, we took a day to head to the volcano on the big island and see the lava flows. We knew that it was going to be a difficult hike in and out, but we really didn't think it through. I'm not sure why. I hope it's not just because we were terrible parents but that might have been the case. It was about a two-mile hike each way. Our plan was to take off in the late afternoon, arriving at the lava flow about dusk, and then heading back as it started getting dark using our flashlights.

Our 3 kids, Carly, Kyle, and Troy, saw to it that the water we *did* have was gone very quickly. Our good friends shared their snacks with us, but everyone was still complaining by the time we arrived at the lava. As we headed back, I started to worry a bit, and when the batteries of our flashlights started to dim, I knew we were in trouble.

We were able to see other hikers, but in the dark we still lost the path. If you have been there yourself, or know what a lava flow looks like, you will know that each step was a big gamble without a flashlight. We had a lot of scrapes, blood, and a good amount of pain and crying, but we eventually made it. If I knew at the beginning what I knew at the end, I would have either prepared much better or not gone at all.

First Things First

The first thing that I remember blowing me away when I began my study in Ephesians was God's promise in chapter 3, verse19. He promised, through the love of Christ, to fill me with love and power. I heard in that verse God promising to give me the life that I had always wanted, the life that I had been striving for. And God forced my hand a bit as I read it. He wanted an answer. Did I *really* believe that He could provide it? My honest answer was, "I don't know, but I sure hope so."

In every Rocky movie, the main character comes to the crossroads. He weighs the prize he is aiming at against the cost of moving forward. And now it's your turn to make that decision. And, make it you must because you are considering going down the most difficult road known to man. But it can also be the most thrilling.

You must decide now to commit yourself to this journey because you are going to want to quit a million times. You are going to say to yourself over and over that it just isn't worth it, and if you don't answer this now, once and for all, you won't make it.

Do you believe that God actually holds fullness of life? Do you believe that God offers what you truly, truly want?

The Other Side of the Same Coin

Paul also tells us in Ephesians 3:19 that experiencing the love of Christ is the key to finding that life and power. In other words, there is no human being or experience that stands between you and fullness of life and power. Not your wife, who doesn't understand your sexual needs. Not your boss, who disregards you on a regular basis. Not your neighbor, whose dog poops in your yard at least twice a week. No human (or dog) stands between you and fullness of life and power.

I am not saying that other people don't impact your life, but I *am* saying that other people cannot stop you from experiencing the love of Christ and finding the fullness of life and power that comes from God.

This journey we are packing for is not a journey that is guaranteed to run through the town of getting what you want. This journey doesn't guarantee that your wife will change at all, though I believe she most likely will. What this journey guarantees is that God will absolutely join with you and love you and fill you up to a point where you will find fullness of life and power. And that will lead to making your marriage as good as it possibly can get. Is that enough for you? Do you believe that He holds the "best" for you (Isaiah 1:19-20)? Do you believe that the abundant life is a life that ultimately will satisfy you (John 10:10)? Do you believe that no other road leads where you most deeply want to go? These are questions you have to answer.

My resounding yes comes from a strong belief that is seated in both the Word of God and from my own experience. God tells the truth, and His satisfaction satisfies. I have seen God come through in incredible ways and He has satisfied me. He has amazed me at the things He has done in my marriage and in my ministry without me focusing on those things at all. In fact, His word to me was that if I would simply focus on *my* issues, He would begin to work in the other areas of my life, those areas that were very important to me but out of my ultimate control.

Some Indian Jones Action

A third question that Eph 3 asks is found in verse 17. Paul says, "I pray that Christ will be more and more at home in your hearts as you trust in him." "Trusting" is one of those Christianese terms that if we are not careful will lose all meaning to us. So let me put it in the New Roger Revised Version:

May Christ be more and more at home in your hearts, may you get closer and closer to Christ, and may you actually start *experiencing* the love of Christ as you trust in Him, as you do things today with Him that you didn't do yesterday, as you risk, with Him and do the scary things He asks you to do.

The third thing we need to pack for this journey is the willingness to risk. For clarification, let me list some of the risks that God has asked me to take over my ten-year journey:

- To be completely and emotionally honest with God about my frustrations, both with Him and with my life.

- To bring my weaknesses as a man and as a husband to the front burner of my thinking and boldly into my conversations with others.

- To own my moodiness, my addictions, my control and anger issues.

- To make an appointment and begin addressing these issues with a counselor.

- To trust Sue to love me in her own way, rather than making her love me in my way.

- To say that I am sorry sooner and sooner after an argument.

- To turn around and apologize after storming out of the room in the middle of an argument.

- To begin the reconnecting process after an argument and not wait for her to come to me.

You see, there needs to be a pretty large chunk of Indiana Jones in each of us. We need the willingness and courage of Peter to get out of the boat and to try something that might get us a bit wet. I would like to remind you at this point that risk and courage fit you. If you are unsure about that just think about how cowardice feels. Courage will be the opposite.

A Battle Companion

It's been mentioned before, but it needs to be mentioned again, that a true friend is crucial to this journey. Several would be better. To put it simply, a friend is someone you can honestly talk to about:

- Your courage or lack thereof.

- Your motives, good or bad.

- Your emotions, or lack thereof.

- Your passions and your lusts.

True, these friends may be few and far between, but they are there. And they are essential to this journey. Read Ecclesiastes 4:10-12 for yourself. It's all right there. When one falls, who will help him up? How can one stay warm alone? Who will guard your back in battle? There is almost nothing worse that feeling alone, except perhaps feeling alone in a difficult situation.

As men, most of us have this instinctive propensity to want to do things alone. It's the ol' "never ask for directions" idea. We have got to get over that to go down this road. You will absolutely need an outside source of encouragement in order to persevere. If you only see things from your perspective, it will look very bleak at times. But an outside source can help remind you of the goal and help you see the progress you have made.

Discussion Questions for Chapter 7

Besides head knowledge, how have you changed this past year? How about the past 5 years? Was it intentional, something you set out to change? Why did you do it? How did it come about?

Within the context of marriage, if there is one thing about yourself that you'd like to change, what is it? Do you think that it is possible for you to achieve that change? Why or why not?

Is what ways—physically, spiritually, emotionally—do you risk in your daily life? Describe the relationship between risk and growing trust.

Chapter 8

Sex, the Heart of Many Problems

A broken and injured heart
often leads to wrong thinking concerning sex,
producing cowardly choices, not courageous ones.

Run from sexual sin!
No other sin so clearly affects the body
as this one does.
1 Corinthians 6:18

Many men dream of having the most incredible sex life possible. To many, that is the epitome of a great life. Many feel that having a good wife and an incredible sex life would overshadow any other struggle. Many believe that they could get through any difficult day if they knew that their wives were waiting at home to satisfy their every fantasy and desire.

Where do men get that picture in their head? I believe it grew out of a childhood that didn't answer their questions. They needed to know if they had what it took to be a real man. They needed that question answered by their parents, primarily their father. But that question is rarely answered completely by our fallen fathers. Most men didn't hear a consistent and affirming message from their fathers. Many men have no idea what their dads thought or think about them. Many other men knew very clearly that their dads were frustrated or disappointed with them.

Moms can try, but they can never fill the void left by absent or un-accepting fathers. And childhood romances hardly ever end with a fairy-tale ending. So the young man's heart is broken, and he learns that loving with abandon hurts. His inner conclusion is that he doesn't have what it takes to be a man, a message he was set up to accept by the pain of living in a fallen world.

With dad's affirmation absent, and the pain of a real relationship still stinging, magazines and videos look very tempting. Watching a video feels like a simple way to escape pain, but what men are doing is training their hearts and brains to feel and think a certain way, a wrong way, about sex and love. Every image trains your brain and heart and body to expect fantasy instead of reality.

A Visual Exercise

Picture two groups of women before you. The first group is every *real* woman in your life and every real woman you will ever meet. The other group is every image of a woman you will ever encounter, be it TV, internet, billboard, etc.

The average male heart, in a time of ache and need springing from the unanswered question, will look at the group of real woman, and be cautious. He has no idea what they think of him. He has no idea how they will respond to his thoughts and to his needs, so he instinctively and subconsciously pulls back.

On the other hand, the average male heart, in a time of ache and need, will get a completely *different* response from the second group of women. Since the images cannot communicate with him and pose no threat, he will hear what he wants to hear, affirmation. In his mind, subconsciously, every beautiful woman on TV thinks he is handsome. In his mind every woman on the internet thinks he is strong and desirable and wants him. It's no wonder men are drawn to porn. It feels so good to be desired without any effort at all.

The Slowly Developing Problem

Did you steal magazines from your neighbor's garage as a kid? Did you work in a store with pornography? Did you sneak a peek at those magazines every chance you had? Do you find yourself channel surfing looking for scantily clad women? Do you instinctively find yourself looking below the neck at women as you walk by them? You, like many, are painting yourself into a corner. I believe that most men can relate to the statements above. And most think they are doing simply what guys naturally do.

When it comes time to get married, these men figure their problem is over. They hope and believe that their wives will replace the pornography. Their wives will see them as desirable and anytime they want sex it will happen, and they will always feel good about themselves. Do you see the train wreck coming?

Time For Some Honesty

Maybe you struggle here. Maybe, after several years of marriage, it's time to come to grips with some startling and difficult things about you.

I can still remember the conversation that Sue and I had many months ago. She said that she felt pressure from me every time we had a few moments to ourselves. She said that the pressure she felt, to have sex, made her not want to have sex. She asked me to stop putting the pressure on. She asked me to let go of pursuing my own happiness through sex.

I stood there in the kitchen trying to hold it together. I knew she was right, but I couldn't get the words out. I told her I would think about it, and went to get ready for work.

As I headed out to the driveway a bit later, Sue followed me. She knew something was wrong. When she asked about it, I broke down. I started crying like there was no tomorrow. Because inside I wasn't sure there was going to be a tomorrow. Sue was asking me to let go of trying to secure my own happiness, a road I had known for many years. She was asking me to let go of the pressure I was putting on her to have sex.

During the entire drive to work, about fifty minutes, I threw up tears. I didn't know if I was dying or coming to life. It felt more like death, but I knew she was right. I knew that the road to a great marriage had to go down this road of letting go of the wrong thinking and the wrong behavior. It just hurt like crazy.

Since that day, nearly every day, I have struggled to grab God's thoughts and wrestle my incorrect thinking to the ground, trying to give my wife her freedom back, trying to be her brave prince. I haven't been successful in redirecting my thinking every day, but most of them. And I need to tell you that what God is doing in the middle of that is nothing short of miraculous. I thought I was giving up my happiness, but what I am experiencing with God and Sue is nothing short of amazing.

As I look back on the past couple of years, I see how God has asked me to show courage, baby step style, in the area of my sexual thinking and behavior. Here is a short summary of the road that God has coaxed me down.

- Admitting to myself that my thinking about sex was wrong.

- Admitting to my wife that sex played an incorrect role in our marriage.

- Letting go, slowly but surely, of my unrealistic and unhealthy sexual expectations.

- Opening up my eyes and working to see Sue's love for me in other ways.

- Intentionally removing the pressure from Sue concerning sex.

- Letting God meet my deepest needs, and trusting Him to do so.

- Letting sex take a more spontaneous and natural place in our marriage.

I went to battle again last night. After a great day together, I started to feel my dysfunction, my old thinking, welling up inside me. I could feel the old expectations starting to take hold. I felt like I "deserved" some physical reward for our great day together. But I saw what God was doing. Having sex because I *deserved* it was not His goal or my goal.

So I never asked her. A greater good was in my sights. God was calling me to let it go and let it be okay. I could see the two fighters in the ring. I felt God and my healthy heart in the corner behind me. I could see the enemy in front of me, and my goal waiting beyond my enemy. And I saw Sue in a ringside seat watching to see how the fight went.

We went to bed and she asked if I wanted to cuddle. I moved over next to her and held her. She was soon asleep, but the battle continued.

- "If she really loved me she would not have gone straight to sleep."

- "I deserve a woman who appreciates me and all the hard work I put into our relationship."

But I could hear God cheering me on from my corner as I fell asleep.

I woke up about two in the morning and my enemy was ruthless. I came back to my corner and listened to my coach. He reminded me of our goal, and of His presence and awareness of the fight. He reminded me that a relationship focused on sex would destroy itself. So I stayed in the fight and continued to battle my dysfunction. I was asleep again within a half hour.

It is now about 6:30 in the morning and Sue will be getting up soon. I think I'm ready! We will see how I handle our time this morning before she heads to work. Will I be disapproving and controlling? If so, the dysfunction wins. Will I smile, and touch, and laugh? Will my behavior tell her that I love her and appreciated the evening we spent together? If so, then I win. And my heart wins. And Sue wins. And sex will be that much closer to being the beautiful and wonderful part of the marriage that God intended.

Growing the marriage I have always wanted is the hardest thing I have ever done. But the prince is finding his heart and is growing the courage to rescue the princess. They can both see that day coming. They are both very excited and hopeful.

Let Her Choose to Love You

One of the early mistakes I made, which delayed my healing for several years, was the thought that I could simply *reshape* my unhealthy sexual thinking. I figured I would just "pull back" a bit, to quit pursuing it so often, to speak *her* love language more often to compensate for *my* expectations.

I kept on trying to prune my sexual thinking but nothing really changed until the day I took it all off the table. Nothing changed with a portion of my focus on my needs. Everything starting to change when I realized that I was simply being selfish and thinking of no one but myself. Everything started changing when I gave up trying to make my happiness happen. Everything started changing when 100% percent of my effort went to fixing me, not mending Sue. You can't sincerely let someone choose you while still trying to control some of the circumstances. It's impossible.

Think back to Ephesians 3:19 and think again about coming to grips with the fact that no one else and nothing else can bring you fullness of life, except the love of Christ. It wasn't until Sue confronted me on the silent pressure she constantly felt that I saw the connection. I was still trying to provide for my own happiness. God was asking me to trust Him. He was asking me to trust Sue and His work in her.

I have mentioned many "crossroads" in this book. This was the toughest. But it has produced the greatest changes. I challenge you to let it all go. I challenge you to take the whole thing off of the table. I challenge you to completely trust God, to risk with Him, and I believe you will find that He will end up being more and more at home in your heart like never before, satisfying your deepest needs like never before.

Something To Focus On

Have you ever had that silly little trick played on you where someone says not to think about the color red, or not to think about a purple elephant? The obvious struggle is that once it is mentioned, it automatically becomes difficult to not think about it. Well, if we are going to succeed in *not* focusing on sex, we need to focus on something else. In my mind it makes all the sense in the world to focus on what your wife desires the most as opposed to what you desire most. And that would probably be communication.

You and I both have a very clear picture in our minds about how we would love our spouse to think about sex. Well, take those very same principles and apply them to your wife's desires. In other words, serve your wife by pursuing communication the way you want her to pursue sex. Doesn't Ephesians 5:28 tell us guys that we should love our wives the same way we love our own bodies? Well, here you go!

To push this idea just a bit further, let's list some ways we wish our wives would pursue sex. We wish...

- They would come to us and want to do it.
- They would show desire and enthusiasm about it.
- They would be creative and fun with it.
- They would see the same value in it that we do.

Okay, now simply apply those same principles to talking with your wife. You know she would love it. She would probably pass out from the experience. If you were to make this effort to value communication at this level, taking your sexual demands off of the table, she will see it as you loving her the same way Christ loved the church! Christ didn't play "give and take" games. He simply gave 100% of Himself to the church, His bride. And it made her beautiful. And your sacrifice will fuel your wife to become all she was meant to be as your wife.

Let's look at a few more thoughts from Eph 5. First, Christ did not sacrifice for His bride for what *He* got out of it. He did it for her. His motive was pure. Second, it was not something He wanted to do at all. He was fully human, and no human ever looked forward to a painful and humiliating death. Lastly, Christ took the lead. He didn't wait until His bride became beautiful to sacrifice His life. In fact, it was His selfless sacrifice that enabled His bride to become beautiful. Those are some great lessons for us to learn.

If you want to take this idea all the way, find other things that are important to your wife and apply the same basic principle to them. Whether it is a hobby or a friendship with another woman, it doesn't matter. If you make it your priority, your business, to help your wife's dreams come true, with no thought of what you get out of it, miracles will happen.

Back To the Bible

It might be worth your time and mine to spend some quality reading in the Song of Solomon. Take a glance through there and learn about God's view of sex, and God's view of what it looks like to pursue a woman. God is no prude. He made men the way they are for a specific reason. And He made sex pleasurable for a specific reason. There is nothing wrong in celebrating the fact we are sexual beings, but we must pursue that celebration as God prescribes. Any other path is sinful and at the deepest level, dissatisfying.

Discussion Questions for Chapter 8

Do you find yourself comparing your wife to other women? When did it start? What do you imagine the other women saying about you?

What were your general thoughts about sex as a teenager? What were your thoughts about sex going into marriage? How did those thoughts change after being married a few years? How have those changes changed you?

What is your reaction to the statement that women love conversation much like men love sex? What is your reaction to the challenge to enjoy and pursue conversation in the same way you want her to enjoy and pursue sex? Would it be possible for you to pursue conversation without expecting sex in return?

Chapter 9

Anger and Withdrawal

*The Bible calls us to be gentle and strong,
knowing when to choose which.
Dysfunction takes both to the extreme
and cripples marriages.*

----

*Husbands, love your wives
and never treat them harshly.*
Colossians 3:19

My favorite subject at Bible College was Theology Proper, a study of the attributes of God. The study of God is not a set-in-stone curriculum. God is too complex to simply look at Him from one angle and get the complete picture. It is not an exact science for we will never know Him completely. So we look at Him from many, many angles and try to get as complete a picture as possible.

One of the simplest ways to look at the attributes of God is through the very simple lens of His gentleness and His strength. God is gentle and God is strong. Can you see how it would be easy to view the rest of His qualities as being expressions of His gentleness and strength. In other words, His omnipresence, His ability to be everywhere at one time, can be seen as a source of power (fighting many enemies) and as a source of gentleness (comforting many sad souls at once). His love can be seen as a source of strength (as He dies for the sins of the world) and also as a source of gentleness (seeking after that one lost lamb).

We too can be categorized as gentle and strong. But our problem is that we don't automatically have God's balance and maturity, and we go too far with those qualities. Men can often take those two strengths and turn them into ways to punish and hurt others. Our ability to be strong can easily be warped into meanness, hurting others. And our ability to be gentle can easily be warped into withdrawing, in order to avoid or inflict pain.

Our heavenly Father is perfect at remaining in the middle of a conflict and staying gentle. Men, fallen human males, are not. Withdrawing from a difficult situation is a perversion of God's gentleness.

God is perfect at showing His strength without injuring and controlling. We are not. A controlling and mean anger is a perversion of God's strength and the strength He gave to us. Is it not the most difficult thing in the world to stay strong in a difficult situation by remaining gentle?

These may or may not be your problems, but getting angry and/or withdrawing are understood to be the two most common ways that a man deals with relational difficulties.

Discovering Our Weaknesses

One of the most interesting things I have ever done was to rescue a bug from a pool of water and watch it recover from its near-drowning. Usually bugs are so busy moving that you don't get to watch them up close at all. But as it lay there, soaking wet, catching its breath, it didn't care about me at all. I got to watch it get dry, clean itself, and take inventory of its health.

In this chapter our goal is not to cure anger or withdrawal. It's simply to take a look at it, to examine it, to see how it works, and to see if we struggle in those areas. But unlike the bug story above, examining unhealthy reactions is difficult. Unlike the recovering bug, unhealthy relational skills are very difficult to get close to. Most people hide them and protect them with all of their might. That is the bad news. The good news is that admitting and owning the responsibility for anger and withdrawal are huge chunks of the work to be done in order to get down the road of healing.

Let's Get Started

There are times when God asks us to be strong, and there are times when God asks us to be gentle. But we don't want to get hurt, so we move away from a vulnerable position to a less vulnerable position, angry versus a controlled strength, withdrawn versus a vulnerable gentleness.

And both overreactions show a lack of courage to face the difficult situation at hand. When a father seeks to discipline his child and the child reacts harshly with, "I hate you dad," it is much easier to simply get angry and send the kid to his room, as opposed to staying connected and vulnerable. On the other side, when a husband seeks to offer affection to his wife, and she responds coldly with, "that's all you ever think about," it is much easier for the husband to shut down and withdraw, as opposed to staying connected and vulnerable.

The goal has to be to remain in the pain and pursue the good of the other party. With the child, the courageous step would be to stay close, share the pain you feel, stay vulnerable and engaged and pursue relationship and instruction. It may sound like a very feminine reaction but it is surely the reaction that takes the most strength. To get angry and send the kid to his room is the simplest and weakest reaction. Many men, perhaps most men, respond to difficult relational situations with anger, and that is sin. It is dysfunctional and cowardly and does not lead to any kind of quality conclusion.

To remain in the pain and engaged with your wife would be difficult but good. To physically stay close, to share how her response hurt you, and to assure her that your goal was to love her well, is the gentle and godly thing to do, but it is the difficult thing to do. Again, that may seem like the soft and feminine response, but which response takes the most courage and strength? Are you starting to see my point?

The position of courage and strength is always the one that takes the most control and compassion. Remember that the fruit of the Spirit contains self-control and love. We have got to see anger and withdrawal as the weaknesses they are. When we begin to head down either of these two diversions, we think that we are doing the natural thing, the only logical thing that we could do. But as in many instances of sin and cowardice, the natural thing is the weak and wrong thing.

I hope that you now see why I say that *recognizing* anger or withdrawal was the biggest chunk of the work. We think we are justified and logical and correct. I mean, what else are you supposed to do? Stay there and take it? How about, staying there and handling it better?

Why Should I Stay There and Take It?

I believe that the vast majority of women, in the world that I know, want to love their husbands. But women find themselves injured in love and life just like guys do. And they are afraid, just like guys are. But God calls us to lead the way, to show courage first.

What I have discovered is that when my wife gets defensive and appears to be attacking me, it is primarily because she is afraid, not because she is mean. I don't tell you this to let her or other women off of the hook for what they said and how they said it. But I say it to you to help you look beyond what they said, to the cry for help that is behind it. They want us to handle it well, and to help them see that we can be trusted, in order for them to handle it better next time. In other words, women, more than men, need to know their partner is safe, before they can be vulnerable with them. That is why I am asking you to show courage, to go first, and to show your strength by remaining gentle when the conversation gets heated. This area is much like the physical area, men are built to initiate and women are built to respond.

"A gentle answer deflects anger, but harsh words make tempers flare." (Proverbs 15:1) There may be no clearer call to courage. When your wife responds harshly to you, to respond with a gentle answer is nothing short of work. Don't tell me a real man isn't soft and gentle. Only a real man has the strength and courage to stay vulnerable and to respond with a gentle answer. Jesus was absolutely a man's man. His response to those who were crucifying Him was nothing short of amazing strength. "Father, forgive them, for they don't know not what they are doing." (Luke 23:34)

Think of it this way. Remember what Solomon told us about two being stronger? He said your role as your wife's friend is to help her back up when she has fallen. Well, if she is responding to you with harsh tones, she has fallen down in her responsibilities as your partner, and she needs you to help her back up. How do you do that? You do that by responding with a gentle answer and guiding her lovingly to a stronger place.

On the other side of the coin, when we passively and sinfully withdraw from a conflict or difficult situation, we are clearly abandoning our wives in a time of need. This is just as hurtful and does just as much damage as being overly aggressive. Our wives, in a time of deep need, need us to step up to the plate, remain in the game, and show courage.

The Affirmation of the Body

Whenever I teach a spiritual gifts class, I make it very clear that the affirmation of the body of Christ, the church, is the clearest indication of an individual's spiritual gift. Many people desire to have certain talents or gifts and assume they have them when it is clear to everyone around them that they do not. You have all listened to people who believed they could sing, but could not. Many of you have been to Sunday school classes taught by people who believed they were great teachers, but were not. If someone has a gift or talent, it is clear to those around them.

If you are not sure whether you have an anger or passivity problem, just ask those people closest to you. If you are married, ask your wife. If you have children, ask them. They will tell you, unless they are afraid of you. Ask a friend you trust. He will often be better at seeing your weaknesses than you are.

If you discover that you struggle in these areas, I encourage you to start talking with others about them. Have a brutal honesty about them. Own the responsibility for them. And in your conversations about your struggles, you should go in three directions.

First, what are your underlying feelings? In other words, your anger or your withdrawal occurs because you feel other feelings that are too hard to handle. Perhaps embarrassment. Maybe pain or regret. Whichever overreaction is yours, find the core underlying feeling.

Second, as expanded in chapter 4, discuss the events in your life that first caused you to feel those core feelings, events with your parents, your neighbors, your school friends or teachers, your first love, etc. When and how did you learn to run away from those initial hurts, turning to anger or to withdrawal? Remember, it is these honest conversations with people you trust that will lead you to the courage it takes to start to move forward.

Third, as expanded in chapter 5, what baby steps is God asking you to take in order to relearn correct responses to those difficult feelings? God can show you the path back to healthy relationship skills, but He will not bypass step one and two.

Discussion Questions for Chapter 9

When and where do you find yourself slipping out of balance and getting angry or withdrawing? What individuals are impacted in the wake of your slip-ups? Can you recall the time in your life when these struggles began?

Map out the path an argument takes between you and your wife? Try to stay neutral. Where does it start? What would it take to dissolve it right there? What do you think your wife is thinking and feeling as an argument begins? What would it cost you to become a peacemaker in that moment? What keeps you from becoming one?

Chapter 10

A Call to Courage

The time for talk is over.
Courage is just around the corner of resolve.

"What you feel doesn't matter in the end;
It's what you do that makes you brave."—Andre Agassi

A few nights ago Sue was coming to bed and telling me about something that she saw on TV. She was unable to really describe it because she was laughing so hard. I didn't really understand what she was trying to say but I sure enjoyed hearing her laugh. And that was one of my goals early on when I first started this journey, to hear her truly laugh. I knew I had bottled her up somehow and I knew that deep laughter would let me know that she was coming alive again.

Hearing her child-like laughter made me feel like a prince. I felt that, in a small but very significant way, her laughter indicated that I was on the right path. I sensed that I was winning the battle to rescue her from the dragon. The sad but true thing had been that *my* dysfunction was the dragon. But she was now finding freedom to laugh and to live again.

Just the other day she told me, for the first time in many years, that I was fun to be married to. I cry almost every time I tell that to someone. Why? Because of the pain I caused her and because of the thrill of giving her laugh back to her. It is like no other thrill.

Just last night, after a few of hours of fairly intense conversation that looked a lot like a misunderstanding, something good broke through. We were at our wits end, and I was about ready, in anger, to call it quits for the night. All of a sudden, in tears, Sue threw her face into my chest and held me. Wanting us to get along overpowered her fear, and her heart raced to the battlefront. For the next half hour or so I saw a brand new Sue. Her heart was full of courage, saying things she had always thought and felt but had hid and protected. That new woman took my heart to brand new places. It is amazing both the power of the heart and the power of two hearts working together. I fell asleep feeling like a world of possibility was fully open to Sue and me.

Courage to Move Forward

For the most part, this book has been about trying to erase the negative behaviors that come from our dysfunctions. I have challenged you to look back and discover those events that caused you to withdraw from healthy reactions. I have challenged you to enter into conversations with men you trust and to be honest about those events and the pain they caused you. My theory and hope has been that the honesty presented there will produce the courage needed to start undoing that behavior, baby step by baby step. No small feat, but doable with God's help.

My instruction was to focus solely on your issues and to refuse to even consider the ways that your wife needs to change. My opinion is that we need to completely die to ourselves and to our desire to blame someone else's behavior for ours. At that point, our wives will see Christ in us, and discover the fuel they need to deal with their issues and their struggles.

My personal experience was that after about five years of working on my own issues, of healing my own heart, I finally had the footing needed to lean into my wife's heart with love. Before that time it would have been selfish at its core, but after five years of healing, God opened the door to spurring my wife on toward love and good deeds.

I now realize that when Sue and I got married, I became a primary tool that God could use to minister to Sue and to help her become all that God wanted her to be. Full of dysfunction, I was a tool that was dull and broken and would do more damage than good in her life. I needed to be fixed and sharpened in order to be powerful in her world.

God's goal was to build a healthy team and to move forward in wonderful ways for the Kingdom, and against the gates of hell. If all we do is look inside and keep trying to make ourselves better and better, never ministering to the world around us, then we have become a perpetual child, self-absorbed and of little value to God.

I see four huge areas of frontier that God wants us to courageously move into as men, once our hearts are heading in the right direction. God wants us to intentionally move forward with Him, with our wives, with our kids, and with His church. Let's look at each one briefly.

Courage With God

Women tend to be better than men in building relationships. Thus women more naturally and intentionally build a relationship with God. I find that most men are very passive in this, and I find that tendency in myself as well. It just doesn't come natural to me to want to pursue God's heart through pursuing time alone with Him. But the Bible calls us to pursue God, to pursue His Word, to grow our relationship with Him intentionally.

It will not come easy. It will take courage and energy and time, but it is absolutely central. To pursue intimacy with Him is to pursue success in every way that God defines it. And this will include our marriage of course. If we abide in the vine, we will bear much fruit. This point cannot be overstated. This entire book as been about battling dysfunction and healing our hearts and marriages, but underneath the entire process has to be a growing relationship with God, which needs to be continually pursued with courage.

My simple encouragement and instruction to you, as stated earlier, is to let your relationship with God be unique. Don't try to copy someone else's relationship. Don't go down anybody else's road. What does God want the two of you to look like? That's a question I believe you should ask Him. If you try to do what someone else is doing it won't fit you and it will feel stale. The reason most our relationships with God are boring is because we are falling into the same old rut of doing our devotions like someone else. Yes, it will include the truth of God's Word, and yes it will involve prayer, but beyond that it needs to be something that you and God develop together.

God is not boring. If our time with Him is consistently boring, then I would say that something is wrong. I'm not saying it needs to be a mountain-top experience every day, but if you dread getting alone with God, something is wrong and needs to be fixed. I would toss out all of your preconceived ideas, and carve out some time, sit down with Him, ask the question, "God, what should our time together look like?"

Courage With Our Wife

Once we get our dysfunctions to a healthier place, our wives are to be courageously pursued in a vast number of ways: her passions, her hobbies, her friendships, and her ministries, just to name a few.

We have a funny line around our place that Sue and I throw out for fun every once in awhile, "Happy wife! Happy life!" As I pursue Sue's happiness, I am deeply satisfied, in ways much deeper than sex. God calls all of us husbands to love our wives deeply. If we obey Him, and accomplish any level of that command, we will know His joy and satisfaction, and that is as good as it gets.

Our dysfunction tends to keep us focused on ourselves, but as we heal, we will find the strength to focus on our wives and be of real help and support to them. In Ephesians 5 we are told that Christ's death on the cross allowed His bride, the church, us, to become lovely through forgiveness and sanctification. We are to play Christ's role in our wives lives. Is your wife becoming more and more lovely because of your sacrifices of love for her? Are her passions growing because of your involvement in her world? Is she enjoying her hobbies more because of your growing support? Are you joining her in praying for and supporting her ministries? No, our wives are not automatically or completely balanced in their world. But that must not keep us from loving them in tangible ways that make their world blossom more and more.

And there will be those times that God will want to use you in helping her become like Him. Being committed to *all* of her world will open the door for her to hear God's instruction through you. But if that is the only time you lean into her world, it will be difficult for her to hear God's voice through you.

Your wife needs you as a teammate. Not just for what the two of you do together, but also for those things that are in her world. Happy wife! Happy life!

Courage With Our Kids

Most women would say that there is nothing more attractive and endearing than watching their husband play with their children or helping them with their homework. I doubt if that is coincidence.

Colossians 3:21 tells us not to aggravate our kids. We aggravate them by being too passive or too harsh. If we withdraw from them, physically, emotionally, and/or verbally we will aggravate them and lose an opportunity to love our wives through them. If we are harsh and impatient with them, we will aggravate them as well, and, again, lose an opportunity to minister to our wives through them.

Children are not simply opportunities to impress our wives, but let's not ignore the benefits either. The Bible tells us about rewards all the time. Let's not be fools and say that the rewards that God has naturally built into the system are not important. If they are not important, He wouldn't have mentioned them in His instructions to us. If you want to build a great marriage, full of respect and love, then pursuing the kids is a must.

It is obviously a must for the children's benefit as well. Let's not forget that a key reason that many of us struggle with dysfunction is because our earthly father was either too passive or too harsh. I'll never forget the look on my son's face when I lost my temper with him when he was just 3 or 4 years old. The look on his face was sheer terror. But the worst part was when I recognized myself in his face, from 45 years earlier, afraid of *my* father. It takes courage to break that cycle.

After a long day at work, I struggle with passivity in dealing with my kids. I come home, hoping to relax and forget about everything as I turn the TV on. But twenty feet away in the kitchen Sue is getting dinner ready and helping the kids with their homework. What we all need to realize is that the kids are learning all right, but not just by doing homework. They are watching and learning about being a father. And they need to see us rerouting our energy away from the TV and into their lives.

My struggle with being harsh has already been mentioned, but I would also like to relay the remedy that I have started to employ with my kids. When I lose my temper with them and come across harsh, I find myself separating myself from them physically and emotionally. I thought that for them to really learn from what they did wrong (the wrong that I had overreacted to) that they needed to see me remain upset even after the punishment was over. (The same dysfunctional thinking I was using with Sue.) I figured this would really make my point with them.

But after analyzing it, I realized two things. (1) fear was at the core of remaining upset, and (2) after the punishment was over, I needed to return to being soft with them. That is what God would do with me after His discipline and after my repentance. In fact, in the definition of the word, justification, after the sin is forgiven, the offender is to be treated as if he *had never sinned*. Let's show our kids a correct picture of God's discipline and love. And if we get it wrong, let's be man enough to apologize.

Courage in Our Church

So far in this book we have stayed very close to home. We have focused on our emotional health as demonstrated primarily in our relationships with our wives and kids. It may seem a bit odd that in this last chapter I would jump over the fence and start dealing with relationships outside the home, but it does need to be touched on. With that said, I believe that if we are not reaching beyond our home and impacting our world for Christ, we are not in balance.

This is a very complicated issue and it would take a book or two to wrestle with both the cause and the cure, but we do need to show courage in pursuing our role in God's Kingdom beyond our own household. True, some men over-involve themselves in church work because they want to cover up their inner struggles, but a greater percentage of men withdraw from the church. And the women around them pay the price. They end up having to fill roles in the church they were never meant to fill. And they lose respect for the men in their lives who fall prey to this fear.

On the positive side of it, the church desperately needs to see men with hearts that are alive and open to people. The church needs to see who are passionate about life and God. In my own life and ministry, it seems like people around me actually believed I had something worth listening to once I started being honest about my struggles. And when people started seeing the changes in my life, doors of ministry really started opening up.

Our wives and kids need to see us love the local church and serve it with passion and balance. This can only take place after we wrestle with our dysfunction and fears and grow a healthy and powerful heart.

In Closing

Five years ago I had very little feelings, not even for my wife. Today I am beginning to feel the things I ought to feel, and enjoying the things I ought to enjoy. Today I tend to cry at the right things: the pain I put my wife through, a hurting friend, a confrontation I fear, etc. I am asking you to join me in learning to become your wife's prince.

- She is held captive by your fear of not being in control.
- She is held captive by your addictions.
- She is held captive by your unrealistic sexual expectations.

- She is held captive by your arrogance that needs to believe that she is less than you are in some way.

- She is held captive by a dysfunctional anger that pins her down and holds her back in so many ways.

- She is held captive by your unwillingness to risk for fear of being embarrassed in some way.

- She is held captive by your secret life that daily steals your heart's desire for her.

Do you believe that God holds out abundant life for you? Do you believe that He holds in His hands those things that satisfy more than the dysfunctional fears listed above? Do you have the courage to start admitting which statements listed above are *your* issues?

If you do, then you can start today. Remember, courage is not the strength to do everything, or anything, but simply to do the *next* thing.

Maybe today is the day. Your princess is waiting.

Discussion Questions for Chapter 10

Describe your relationship with God in a few statements of brutal honesty. What kind of a relationship would you like to have with Him? If your relationship with Him were tailored just for you, what kinds of things would it include?

Give some specific examples of what it would look like to intentionally and aggressively support your wife's passions, hobbies, friendships, or ministries?

Describe your best moments of the week with each of your kids. Is it embarrassing to do so for any reason? What would it look like to pursue each of them?

Are you actively involved in a ministry in your local church? Do you dread your commitments or look forward to them? From your example, what are the positive and negative things your kids are learning from you about serving God in the local church?

LaVergne, TN USA
01 April 2011
222581LV00003B/1/P